Aboli...

A play by

Gabriel Gbadamosi

Abolition

First published in 2023 by flipped eye publishing
Under the defeye series | www.flippedeye.net

© 2023 Gabriel Gbadamosi

The right of Gabriel Gbadamosi to be identified
as the author of this work have been asserted by him in accordance with
the Copyright, Designs and Patents Act of 1988.

1 2 3 4 5 6 7 8 9 10

ISBN 9781905233670

A CIP catalogue record for this book is available from the British Library.

Jacket design by Ahmed Akasha | www.d237.com

This book is typeset in Book Antiqua and Palatino Linotype

Printed and bound in Great Britain.

Supported using public funding by
**ARTS COUNCIL
ENGLAND**

ABOLITION

GABRIEL GBADAMOSI

With thanks to Debbie Seymour, Sibylla Wood and Bonnie Greer

CAST of *ABOLITION*

In order of appearance

The SURGEON, Mr Jones
The PURSER, Tom
The CAPTAIN, John Knox
The BOSUN, Mr Palmer
A SLAVE
The CABIN-BOY, part of the CREW
John TARLETON, a Liverpool Merchant
JAKE, Knox's Slave
The NEGER SHANTYMAN, part of the SHANTY CHORUS
William FOX, Quaker
William WILBERFORCE, MP (for Hull)
CROWD Scenes, the MOB
MAN, at the Cock-Fight
JENNY, Tarleton's Daughter
FIDDLER, part of the Press-GANG
William PITT, the Younger, Prime Minister
Archibald BALZIEL, a Bristol Captain

PROLOGUE

The Dead List

Cabin of the Blackamoor Jenny. *TOM writes in the ship's book. The SURGEON dictates, cleaning and gathering his bloody tools into a bag.*

SURGEON: ... Nicholas, before the mast, with an Intermittent Fever. Mr Young, apprentice Sail-maker, with a Bilious Fever. The Armourer – died. The Cook – died. The Carpenter, with a Head-Ache, but refused Medicine – died. Jack Reynolds – died. Jack Strahan, with a Diarrhoea. Harry, with the bloody Flux. The boy Peter – died.

The SURGEON stops, gazing in air, as if trying to remember someone. TOM waits a moment.

TOM: Should we not record the Cause of Death in all Cases?

SURGEON: By all means, Purser. Your Guess.

TOM: Does that complete the Dead List?

The SURGEON gestures for him to continue writing.

SURGEON: To date. March 5th, 1792. Arrived at our

> Moorings at the Mouth of the Niger with 47
> crew. In three Weeks of our Stay on the Coast,
> 11 sewn in their Hammocks and committed.
> And a further 7 took ill with Exhaustion
> and Fever. The Rump of our Crew-Men
> stalked by the Yellow Jack ... A murderous
> Fellow, somewhat shadowy in Appearance;
> his Attack made even more terrible by the
> ivory-yellowness of his Skin and Teeth, and
> the suddenness of Death on his Approach ...
> Officers of the After-Guard being, of course,
> exempt.

TOM has stopped writing. He crosses out the last words and turns the book toward the SURGEON.

TOM: Sign here.

The SURGEON takes the pen and signs. The CAPTAIN enters.

SURGEON: ... Mr Jones, Surgeon ...

CAPTAIN: What's this?

TOM: Drawing up the Dead List, Sir.

CAPTAIN: Waste Work! The Cargo's not complete. I want
                  my Men up and doing.

SURGEON: The Dead?

CAPTAIN: Sarcasm, Surgeon? Your Knife were better
                  honed in finding Cures.

SURGEON: The best Cure's to be away on open Sea. The
                  Crew need Air, and Food, and Rest; to be better
                  provisioned and out of the way of the Coast.
                  This is hopeless.

CAPTAIN: No Work, no Food. We go nowhere without a
                  full Haul.

SURGEON: You can't Starve sick men.

CAPTAIN: You argue with me?

SURGEON: Without a Crew, Captain, we're stuck.

The CAPTAIN strikes down the SURGEON, wounding him in the head.
TOM, shocked, instinctively bends to him.

CAPTAIN: Leave him! Die, and be damned!

TOM hesitates, then disobeys. He helps the SURGEON back onto a chair.
The SURGEON takes a swab from his bag and holds it to the wound. He looks
at the CAPTAIN.

SURGEON: Not dead, Capt. Knox, Sir ... You may chance to
                       need me yet.

TOM: *(To the CAPTAIN)* Sir, with Sickness, depletion
                       of our Stores, no Slaves to buy at the Factories
                       and none being brought down to them, we
                       cannot wait much longer. It's my Duty as
                       Purser to tell you so. We must make a Decision:
                       Stay or Go. What will you do?

CAPTAIN: What more Slaves do we need to make us
                       profitable?

TOM: Another 60. We have 286, or thereabouts. With
                       no further Losses we could meet costs. Should
                       Sickness begin to rot our Cargo at the same
                       Rate as the Crew, it would be a losing Voyage.
                       For you, and my Uncle.

CAPTAIN: Show me the Account. *(To the SURGEON)* Go
                       examine the Negroes aboard, what State they're
                       in. Report how many can make the Crossing. I'll
                       decide what's needed.

The CAPTAIN turns to inspect the ship's accounts. The SURGEON throws
down his swab and rises shakily, still bleeding from the Head.

TOM: Are you up to it?

SURGEON: I have my Doubts.

11

The SURGEON takes up his bag, and looks at TOM.

                        Do you?

TOM: I doubt you were made for this Trade. I cannot
                        afford to doubt myself.

SURGEON: The Slaves are waiting.

The CAPTAIN turns.

CAPTAIN: Keep your Head, Mr Jones. And I may give you
                        the Chance to mend it.

*The SURGEON goes. TOM sits back with the ship's accounts. The CAPTAIN
paces.*

TOM: As of now, it's clear the *Jenny* must make a
                        losing Voyage.

The CAPTAIN kicks over a chair.

                        Our Hands are bound by the Factories: their
                        Prices, Slaves scarce. We cannot trade freely in
                        anything with the Natives. In my Opinion, she
                        must always make a losing Voyage.

CAPTAIN: As for your Opinion, Purser, give me Facts!

TOM: On current Prices, a Short-Fall of above 100
                        Pound Sterling.

The CAPTAIN paces in thought. TOM closes the book.

                        Bound to be a losing Voyage.

CAPTAIN: Bound? Bound where? Bound to a Profit for
                        any further Command! Bound to nothing! Open
                        the Book! I'll bind her 'fore she leaks my Profit!

TOM opens the book.

                        Aye, Bound, with one Bound for Home, and
                        home on Profit! What Wages?

TOM looks.

TOM: Four hundred in Spanish dollars; 400 in Pound
                               Sterling on our Return to Liverpool.

The CAPTAIN paces.

CAPTAIN: Subtract for Deaths.

TOM: We pay Wages for the Dead.

CAPTAIN: Then we plank the Sick down on the West
                               India Wharfs with half their Pay. How lightens
                               that the Standing of our Profit?

TOM: The Crew's contracted for a Return Voyage.

CAPTAIN: Profit's what we carry Home – and no Man
                               comes on Freight!

TOM: Their contract is for Half – the better Half, in
                               Sterling – on our Return. We can't plank down
                               half-Dead. Our Crew's depleted as it is.

CAPTAIN: There's ten strong Men for every One that's
                               Gone, to take up Slack and haul a Passage
                               home!

TOM closes the book.

TOM: The Balance of their lives thrown in for Profit?

Banging and shouts from offstage; they turn to the sound.

BOSUN *(off)*:   They strike, damn you! Close it, shut the Hatch!

*TOM and the CAPTAIN pass from the cabin to the deck. They meet the
BOSUN dragging a SLAVE, handcuffed and thumb-screwed in praying
position, both legs shackled and stumbling. The BOSUN pulls on the chain
attached to a collar about the neck. There is a grille over the head, open at the
mouth, making the SLAVE faceless.*

TOM: *(To the BOSUN)* What's here?

CAPTAIN: Learn by Example, what is Customary to do.
Stand back.

BOSUN: They won't eat.

The BOSUN stands behind, forcing back the head, and inserts a speculum oris (a vice with forward blade and backward hooks) into the SLAVE's mouth.

The Thumb-Screw's to take out the
Stubbornness. This opens his Mouth. Stand
back. *(Forces it open)* Grub's up. Our Promise:
we won't eat you.

The SURGEON enters, drenched in sweat – his head still bloody and his shoes are off. The soles of his feet leave prints of blood across the deck. He approaches and pulls open an eye of the SLAVE, lifts and drops the jaw and examines the rusted chain around the neck, finding a chafed wound.

SURGEON: This isn't Hunger. It's Locked-Jaw.

TOM sees the SURGEON's feet, and looks at the trail of blood across the deck.

TOM: Where are your shoes?

SURGEON: It's Impossible to go amongst them with my
Shoes on – they lie so close together I should
have hurt them if I did. I have the Mark upon
my Feet of Skin and Blood, of Effluence, the
Putrefaction of their lying in the 'Tween-Decks.

CAPTAIN: What Condition are they in? Can they make the
Crossing?

SURGEON: Am I to re-create Man from Slime? I cannot do
it!

A Silence. The CABIN-BOY appears, also silent. TOM looks uneasily about. He speaks in a whisper.

TOM: Quiet, the Men are listening …

SURGEON: I have known them go down well, and in the
Morning be brought up Dead. I have sat by

the Gratings and felt the Burst of Heat and Suffocation from their Rooms, as if I sat by a Fire in the Torrid Zone. It is the most horrid Sight I have ever seen. It is the Deformation of Flesh, a Vat of Blood and Mucus. It is the Boiling Coast ...

TOM: *(To the CAPTAIN)* It's the knock on the Head.

BOSUN: This is Disobedience.

SURGEON: This is Hell!

The CAPTAIN hesitates, a moment of indecision. They watch him. He pushes aside the SURGEON and turns to the BOSUN.

CAPTAIN: Unlock the Armoury, Bosun. Give every Man his Gun. I'll wait no more on the Factories. A Bounty of One Guinea for every Negroe captured, to be shared among the Crew. We sail tonight on the Land-wind.

TOM: This Action is illegal!

CAPTAIN: I am the Law here! Beyond my Word's the Coast – where there is no Law, only Banished Men. *(To the CREW)* Take Action to defend the Ship! We can Save ourselves and be out at Sea by Morning! One Guinea!

The CAPTAIN looks at the SLAVE slumped on the deck.

Clear that off the Deck. Make ready!

The ship's bell rings for action. The CAPTAIN goes. The CABIN-BOY gives his shoulder to the SURGEON and leads him away. The BOSUN takes hold of the chain and drags the SLAVE past TOM.

BOSUN: Look to me as we go. There's no-one looking over our Shoulder when we set Foot there. No Classes of Men at all. Only those who don't know what Hell is, or don't believe in it. Or don't believe they're in it.

The BOSUN drags away the SLAVE.

TOM: We Steal, by Force.

He goes, the bell ringing.

SCENE ONE

Blackamoor Jenny

JOHN TARLETON, merchant, and Captain JOHN KNOX – a surly air of being distracted from his account book by his employer. Quayside – hogsheads, dry barrels, etc. being loaded by jib. Hawkers' cries – 'Round & Sound 5 pence a Pound', 'Lights for the Cat, Liver for the Dogs', 'Buy my fat Chickens', etc.

TARLETON: I have myself Overseen the provision. How do you find her?

KNOX: How many African Voyages has the Ship made, Mr Tarleton?

TARLETON: The *Jenny*? This is her fifth. She's seaworthy, Captain Knox. All 200 ton of her. Built here on the Mersey.

KNOX: She seems solid.

TARLETON: Trust to your own Inspection.

KNOX: Aye. Before I sail.

TARLETON: In what Season of the Year did you usually sail, Captain Knox?

KNOX: I attempted to get in before the Hurricane Months.

TARLETON: The healthy Season?

KNOX: In the Western Ocean I hardly know one Season more healthy than another.

TARLETON: The Hurricane Months are not the most unhealthy?

KNOX: That is the sickly Season.

TARLETON: What is your opinion? By making this Passage now, will our Loss in Sickness not be greater?

KNOX: In crossing the Atlantick it is always equally unhealthy.

The CABIN-BOY enters, and drops a small chest of KNOX's. A bible falls open among the papers.

KNOX   *(Hard)* Put that down easy!

The CABIN-BOY kneels to reload the chest on the quay. KNOX goes over and picks up the bible open to the page.

                    (Reads) "The Waters are come into my Soul. The Sorrows of Death compass me. The Floods of the Ungodly make me afraid." *(Nods)* That's apt. *(To the CABIN-BOY)* You can't drop things, Boy. Not at Sea. Why, you'd lose a Leg, or an Arm. Or, d'you see ...?

KNOX shows him a hand with a finger missing.

                    The Fingers on a Hand.

He allows the finger back into place. The CABIN-BOY stands with the chest; KNOX replaces the bible on top; the CABIN-BOY goes. KNOX returns to his accounts.

TARLETON: A firm and a fair Hand, Captain Knox. But not, I trust for my Benefit?

KNOX: I am not in the Habit of disregarding my Employer, Mr Tarleton.

TARLETON: Why did you leave your Bristol Employer?

KNOX: My last Ship took Water.

TARLETON: You lost her?

KNOX: In the Estuary. She had more Holes than a
                         Sieve, or a Dutchman's Cheese. I lost my
                         Stockings, not my Nerve.

TARLETON: The *Blackamoor Jenny* has more at stake, Sir,
                         than the Insurance Money. Your Purser is a
                         Nephew of mine.

KNOX: Your Nephew?

TARLETON: His name's Tom. He'll be taught the Trade and
                         make an Inspection of our Holdings in the
                         West India Islands. He is the more substantial
                         Investment, Captain Knox, than either you or
                         the Ship.

KNOX: He comes at your own Risk.

TARLETON: No, Sir, at yours. Bring him back, Captain. It's
                         worth your next Voyage, for me, or any other
                         Ship-Owner of Liverpool.

KNOX: I'm lacking still a Bosun, a Carpenter, a
                         Sailmaker, and a Cook.

TARLETON: The Company keeps a Register of Debtors to be
                         found in the various Inns. You may call on them
                         to discharge their Debt – with the assistance of
                         Bailiffs.

JAKE enters, and looks at KNOX.

KNOX: *(To JAKE)* Get you aboard.

TARLETON: Your Boy?

KNOX: He comes with me. At my own Risk.

TARLETON holds a Guinea out to JAKE.

TARLETON: *(To JAKE)* Here's a Guinea waits for you. Watch over your Purser. His Mother wants him back with his five white Limbs intact.

KNOX: Keep your Guinea, Mr Tarleton. He'd spend on a Whore, and not bring back the Change. And that's a poor Guarantee for your Nephew.

TARLETON: Your Negroe is one thing, Captain Knox, my Nephew another. Bring him back. And knock some Sense into your Boy: he could purchase the Pox for a Farthing.

TARLETON goes.

KNOX: Where do you wander?

JAKE: The Streets.

KNOX: In Pursuit of what?

JAKE does not respond.

Put your Face to the Ocean. If you have done any Filth in this Town, let what is to come, come now – before we sail – for all the Intermediate Space is Loss and utter Worthlessness.

JAKE lowers his head.

Remember, you, the Psalmist: "There is no Rest in my Bones because of Sin. My wounds stink, and are Corrupt. My Loins fill with a loathsome Disease, and There is no Soundness in my Flesh."

JAKE: I followed the crowd.

KNOX: For what?

JAKE: To be near them. Men, Children, Women spat on me – swore.

KNOX: When I plucked you from a Slave Hole, up
                  from a horrible Pit, out of the Mire of your
                  Heart, put Clothes on your Back, formed you,
                  fed you, fenced you from Sin – was it for the
                  Roaring of a Mob?

JAKE: They set on me! Do I pray? I wanted to Curse!

KNOX: Put your face to God, there is the Roaring of an
                  Atlantick. Pray you recover your Self, before
                  you go Hence, and be no more.

JAKE: There is no Safety – *(Grasping his hand and arm)*
                  – if I am Alone.

KNOX: Who is not? *(Withdrawing his hand)* You were
                  born Alone, onto a dark-locked Ocean. By
                  assaying the Weights, Measure and Cables
                  of your Self, you make a Mast and Quadrant
                  of your Soul to skirt the howling of an
                  Unregenerate Will. Submit to the tempted,
                  agonised, crucified, Incarnate Christ: the
                  purifying Impulse of the Sea – and take the
                  Measure of your Days, how short a Chain they
                  are to plumb that Depth of Mystery.

JAKE: I do believe it, feel it – I do hope for it, I cry for
                  it with my Breath!

*The SURGEON enters with bottles of spirit; the CABIN-BOY carrying the
SURGEON's tools.*

SURGEON: I prefer the Enthusiasm of Bottled Spirits.

KNOX looks up.

KNOX: How's that, Surgeon; on the Rum so soon?

SURGEON: It fires the Breath against a foggy Ocean,
                  Captain. Besides, my Sweet-Tooth's playing up.
                  It soothes the Pain.

KNOX: Why then apply your Tools to it.

21

SURGEON: I'd rather bite this Bullet in the Bottle-Neck. *(To JAKE)* Any Ailments, Jake?

CAPTAIN: None you'd cure. Your Cabin-Boy's not been to Africa before. *(To the CABIN-BOY)* Go, submit yourself to the good Doctor.

The CABIN-BOY drops a large pair of tongs with a clang.

CABIN-BOY: God give me Health to keep away from him!

SURGEON: That barbarous Climate strikes you dead at whim!

The SURGEON goes aboard.

KNOX: *(To the CABIN-BOY)* Keep your Eye on the Pier-Head. You won't be seeing it for long. Slaving's an uncertain Business.

NEGER SHANTYMAN *(off)*:   Give it a Song, there, Captain?

KNOX: Aye, go on!

KNOX takes his accounts and goes aboard.
The CABIN-BOY looks at JAKE, backs away and goes aboard.

NEGER SHANTYMAN/SHANTY CHORUS *(off)*:

> *The Guinea-Man's nailed to the Slaver's Ship-Mast*
> *T'me, way, ay, and blow the man down,*
> *It's growl if you may, but go if you must*
> *O, gi' me some time to blow the man down!*

> *Blow the man, down, Johnny, kick a man down*
> *Johnny, way, ay, and blow the man down,*
> *Drag a man down, right down to the ground*
> *O, gi' me some time to blow the man down!*

JAKE: Go where you must – Go alone.

JAKE turns from the ship and runs off.

SCENE TWO

Paradise Street

NEGER SHANTYMAN:

> *It's as I was walkin' down Paradise Street*
> *T'me, way, ay, and blow the man down,*
> *A six-foot-six Neger I happened to meet*
> *O, gi' me some time to knock a man down!*

Paradise Street, Liverpool – hawkers and street gamblers. WILLIAM FOX and WILLIAM WILBERFORCE enter; FOX purchases a song-sheet being sung by the NEGER SHANTYMAN, and catches up with WILBERFORCE.

> *Ye'll know me again when y'Money's all spent*
> *Says he, way, ay, and knock a man down,*
> *Be Chains on me Ankles an' Horns on me Head*
> *O, gi' me some time to blow the man down!*

WILBERFORCE: Is Repentance bought for a Song in the Street? Or why this public Sermon? Liverpool is not the place for it.

FOX: I must speak.

WILBERFORCE: Then speak in Parliament.

FOX: It is here in Liverpool they must hear me.

WILBERFORCE: You breathe its foul Air, Mr Fox. What is this Place?

FOX:	Paradise Street, an open Brothel. Resort of every Cut-Throat and Cut-Purse that was not admitted to a Place in Parliament.
WILBERFORCE:	Quite the Maiden speech; am I your Procurer, Mr Fox?
FOX:	You obtain me my Seat, Mr Wilberforce.
WILBERFORCE:	Your Procurer?
FOX:	Tell me: am I to act as my Conscience dictates, or as your Place-Man? One more among a pack of Cut-Throats clamouring for Preferment?
WILBERFORCE:	You have a low view of the House.
FOX:	Is it not a Place where Men are bought and sold?
WILBERFORCE:	The House … is an honourable Estate. Which is rotten; the very Planks wormed and rotten with Place-Men put there to gnaw at their own Scaffold. Not a Brothel, Mr Fox; a Corpse. And some would keep it hung that way till it be Corrupt – not superficially, against the Skin, but radically, and to the very Core. We come with this Election to a kind of Cross-Roads. I'd take down that Corpse and make it walk.
FOX:	Then worm out the Place-Men.
WILBERFORCE:	Do you imagine they have no Masters? They do. Whereas here, I imagine, they serve themselves.
FOX:	Jack Tars, Wharf-Hangers, hulks of Seamen cut off at the Knee. A Pardon for the Pox. A Pardon for any poor Pluck-Scab. Put out the light and let 'em to it – with my Prayers. But the People who damned this Place with the Blotch of Slavery I do not forgive.

WILBERFORCE:	You take the Bull by the Horns –
FOX:	It is a Blade in my Breast; I am offended.
WILBERFORCE:	But when you take your Sermon to the Docks – will that Mob not snort its Virulence in your Face? Do you know what Passions you arouse? Do you own a Slave? Have you Money staked? Ever knocked a Negroe into the Hold? Or do you simply wish to pit your Passion against theirs? These Conflicts should be resolved, and tempered, through Change – peaceful Change, not violent Enthusiasms.
FOX:	There is Revolution in France, ferment in England. We must respond to Change. The Time is ripe to press home, more forcibly, our Charge of Corruption against the Slaving Lobby.
WILBERFORCE:	If we profit from the Unrest, the Emotions of the Moment, it is dangerous to be seen leading them. Dangerous and damnable. No, Mr Fox, it is in the Nature of Dissent to overstate its case.
FOX:	It is the Vice to understate it.
WILBERFORCE:	The Slave Trade must end, but the Rational Order of things must be preserved. Property in the Slave is untenable, but Property is still the Corner-Stone of any stable, Christian Society. I give you, that's hardly a Sermon for the Poor of the Docks. Now, which way?
FOX:	Over there – Canning Place, the Custom House. That way, Wapping Dock, Salthouse Dock, and beyond George's Dock, the Mersey Bar.
WILBERFORCE:	Then let's go. Let's go see an African ship.

Whore on the Water

In the changing crowd, the NEGER SHANTYMAN passes again by the docks.

NEGER SHANTYMAN:

> *Ripe in me pocket and drunk on me feet*
> *T'me, way, ay, blow the man down,*
> *A Pock-Black old Judy I happened to meet*
> *O, gi' me some time to blow the man down.*
>
> *Her Tackle was rotten, and O! down below*
> *T'me, way, ay, blow the man down,*
> *Rags on her Main-Mast an' Blood in her Hold*
> *O, gi' me some time to blow the man down!*

WILBERFORCE:	What, all? All these ships? Slavers?
FOX:	Guineamen, all of them.
WILBERFORCE:	Quite a Fleet. Fine, tall knocking Masts. That Wind creaking in Wood, flapping the Canvas. Tugging at your Sleeve like a crying Woman. It was Shipping made this Country great. Do not forget.
FOX:	And that – hear? – a Pitch above the rest. Tuned to the Wind – a rattling. Silence. They say you hear it above, at the Height of a Storm, the Sea crashing. A Devil's moan tuned to the Mast.
WILBERFORCE:	You do Violence to your Imagination. The Sea is quite calm. Handsome enough Ships; prettily rigged-up. How comes the Devil in it? Slaving is a problem in any Maritime Nation. It can and must be dealt with, if we are to remain strong. It's a flaw we inherit, and deal with, surely, like Sin.
FOX:	*What* is Sin?!

WILBERFORCE: *(A raised eye)* Ignorance of God?

FOX: That Ship – there. What's her Name? Can they hear me aboard?

A cock-fight gathering by the docks gets distracted by FOX; JAKE being furtive.

WILBERFORCE: *(Making out the name)* The Blackamoor ... Jenny.

FOX: Aye. Whore on the Water. And the Waters She sits on are Peoples, and nations, and Multitudes of Tongues crying, *Ah!For Shame! For Shame!* A rush of Voices, heavy and resistless as a Head-long Sea!

That Storm is coming. For see how she lists! A fire-Ship. Her Shrouds catching light, the Pall of her Sails – a Bellows of darkening Fire. And those, stood among the Rigging, Infernals on a fire-Ship, roaring and cursing their God. The Sea reddens and thickens with the Blood she drinks of the Nations, the Innocent, and the Damned.

Ask them, ask them all that Profit from this Trade, and have drunk of Blood from fine Port Glasses, are you Guilty, or not Guilty? Have you not drunken the Whore's Cup here? And marred the Workmanship of God? Instead of saving Man's Lives, destroyed them? You, are you Guilty, or not Guilty?

What do they Plead? That Man – Man that was born in Sin according to the Law – is everywhere in Chains. We it is who but do the Lord's Work. They serve God with their Lips, whom God spewed out of his Mouth!

To deny Man his Perfection, tell him he must have a Body of Sin, and be in his Sin while on Earth, does that not make him Imperfect? Answer it, here, at the Bar! Guilty, or not Guilty?

The bell of a ship's passing the bar. Distant voices of the SHANTY CHORUS, heaving aboard, take their lead from the NEGER SHANTYMAN. They chime in with the ending of FOX's sermon. The dock crowd, distracted by FOX, turns away.

NEGER SHANTYMAN / SHANTY CHORUS *(off)*:

> *It's over the Bar with y'Back fit to bust*
> *T'me, way, ay, and blow the man down,*
> *Growl if you may, but it's go if y'must*
> *O, gi' me some time to blow the man down!*

The bell recedes.

WILBERFORCE: There go some have Missed your Sermon. Give over this Conjuration, it is too Public. Slavery is with us: Man is Sinful. You may save him from his Nature, but that Salvation is a process. I wish your Voice to make it a Parliamentary one.

The Cock-Fight

Hue and Cry from the MOB as the distracted cockfight turns on JAKE, grappled by his arms, struggling. A MAN scratches bloody cockspurs across his face.
                 (To FOX) Come away!

FOX stands his ground and looks directly into the forward thrust of the MOB.

MOB: Turn his Pockets! – Where's the Money? – Hang him!

JAKE is taken by the legs, upended, and shaken.

MAN: Hold him steady! *(To JAKE)* Do I pluck out your Day-Lights, One by One, or do I get a Guinea each?

FOX: His Eyes will cost you.

JAKE is slid to the ground, and held.

MAN: A Thief – he stole from me at the Fight.

FOX: From your pocket?

MAN: Bets off the Floor. Everyone a Drop of Blood
                    from my Beauty.

FOX: Then you must remain out of Pocket. Your
                    Beauty suffer the Loss.

MAN: For a Black Joke?

FOX: Can an Ethiope change his Skin, or the Leopard
                    his Spots? Or you do Good, that are accustomed
                    to Evil?

MAN: Methodist or Magistrate? It's a hanging
                    Offence, and I'll have my Money.

FOX: If took from the Person, not off the Floor.

MAN: Who'll pay the difference? It's enough to hoist a
                    Neger.

FOX: You confuse the Law – that's Murder.

The MOB back off.

MAN: The law belongs to Gentlemen. *(To JAKE)* Keep
                    your Guinea. I catch you again, I'll have it back
                    in Blood.

He goes. FOX looks at the MOB. They disperse.

WILBERFORCE: Well, Mr Fox. To pluck from Riot the Rule
                    of Law is the mark of a Parliamentarian. To
                    salvage this particular Specimen, is the Act of
                    an Apostle.

FOX: *(To JAKE)* You're no Man's Slave. One Foot on
                    English Soil, you're Free. Only a Gallows
                    removes that Foothold.

JAKE remains mute. FOX kneels and reaches into JAKE's mouth, past his grip, and extracts a guinea. He wipes it on JAKE's shirt, and returns it to his pocket.

	For the Ferryman. But it won't do to steal. I'd stake your Life on it, Mr …?
JAKE:	Jake.
FOX:	Are you a Thief, Jake?
JAKE:	A Jake's a Wall let every Man there piss on. Who'd give me the Steam off their Piss if I wasn't? A Thief in good faith – of hot Air, Foul smells, stale Beer, needs Must.

Sound of a thunderstorm approaching.

WILBERFORCE:	*(To FOX)* Time is pressing. Shall we?
FOX:	*(To JAKE)* Stand up. You wrong your Countrymen – though I suspect you for one of us.

WILBERFORCE and FOX go. JAKE takes from his pocket FOX's handkerchief, watch and song-sheet.

JAKE:	Time's pressing. Stand up, for the Ferryman. Here's a Guinea – for your trouble. But it won't do. I'd stake your Life on it. – Sir, What's to stake, when you've to Steal a life?

He runs off, dropping the song-sheet. The NEGER SHANTYMAN enters to gather it up for resale.

NEGER SHANTYMAN: *(Straightening it out, he reads)*

> *The Thief of your Heart is a blade in your Breast;*
> *Pick up from the gutter and go to your rest;*
> *There by the gallows tree.*
> *Despised by a Lover there comes no relief;*
> *Who stole your Body, stole your belief;*
> *There by the gallows tree …*

He lifts an eyebrow, and goes.

SCENE THREE

Jenny and Tom – The Storm

The Tarleton house, Liverpool. JENNY and TOM enter, their outer clothes wet.
A dark storm outside.

JENNY: They're making a Fire in the Study. Put off your
Things here. You must be rather damp.

JENNY flings off her hat, and begins lighting the lamp.

TOM: Not too bad. The storm caught us both – are
you Cold?

She looks at him by lamplight.

JENNY: Yes, you are rather Wet. You may stand in your
Clothes if you want, or you may put them off.

TOM: It is not the Rain I am Conscious of, Cousin; but
your Mood.

JENNY: I am Prone on Days such as this to the most
obscure and inward Reverie. The Rain makes
me Sombre, the heavy Confinement of the
Storm. The Moon also makes its Presence felt. I
become no better than the most Impractical of
Mrs Radclyffe's Gothick Heroines.

TOM: Impractical in so Wet a place as Liverpool.

JENNY pauses, smiles. She takes off her coat. TOM watches. He takes out a necklace, approaches and fastens it about her neck.

I had it engraved. I hope you can like it.

JENNY: You're grown since last we met. Broader about the Shoulders, more assured. Almost a Tarleton; my Father will be pleased.

TOM: Some few Shadows about the Eye, Jenny; but you seem not much older.

JENNY: So, Cousin Tom. How was your Journey up from the Country?

TOM: Tolerable good. The Axle broke, the Coach-Man was drunk, the Passengers, for the most part, kept up a lively conversation of Hands and Eyes.

JENNY: Sorry to hear of your Father's Death. I expect you're worth considerably more a Year. And what of my dear Aunt?

TOM: She's well as can be.

JENNY: Oh?

TOM: My father left some considerable Debts. We are not sure of his Estate. My Mother and I have some private Income …

JENNY: Poor Tom. What then have you come to pawn? A battered Trunk? Your Boots? The Clothes you stand up in? You're too late to redeem your Virginity – I have disposed of that.

TOM: I come to redeem my Credit with my Uncle, not with you.

JENNY: I see. *(Turning away)* I hear he packs you off to Guinea within the week?

TOM:　　　　　　　　Aboard the *Black'moor Jenny*. He's eager I
　　　　　　　　　　master the Reins of his Affairs in the Trade.

JENNY:　　　　　　　*(Turning back)* He's giving you the *Jenny*?

TOM:　　　　　　　　As Purser. I'll breathe and be active on her these
　　　　　　　　　　next Months.

JENNY:　　　　　　　Indeed?

TOM:　　　　　　　　Hardly her Maiden-Voyage, but I've a Mind to
　　　　　　　　　　make her haul for her Money.

JENNY:　　　　　　　You sail very close to the Wind, Cousin. I liked
　　　　　　　　　　your Tact better. Let us not mention some
　　　　　　　　　　question of Taint on your Father's side from
　　　　　　　　　　among those Windy Islands. It's your first
　　　　　　　　　　Voyage, isn't it?

TOM:　　　　　　　　Yes.

JENNY:　　　　　　　A pretty Ship. She's been many times to Africa,
　　　　　　　　　　and straddled the Atlantick. You'll need your
　　　　　　　　　　Wits about you.

TOM:　　　　　　　　What's the Atlantick, for a Fortune coming
　　　　　　　　　　Home again?

JENNY:　　　　　　　You are not his Heir; I am here, and you must
　　　　　　　　　　reckon on me.

TOM:　　　　　　　　Should your father include you in his Inventory
　　　　　　　　　　of Assets, why resent me?

JENNY:　　　　　　　No more – nor less – than any Man who'd want
　　　　　　　　　　control of my Bed. We must see what happens.

TOM takes off his outer clothes. JENNY watches.

TOM:　　　　　　　　Does your Father keep no Eye on who you
　　　　　　　　　　entertain?

JENNY finishes lighting the lamps.

JENNY: The Town is full of Side-Shows. When my
          Father's not profiting by them, he's scheming
          to put them out of Business. As for me, having
          thrown up such a Distance between his Nature
          and mine – a kind of Wilderness of Turn-Stiles
          – he'd hardly notice me gone among them. I am
          used to it. Having grown in the Wilderness of
          his Neglect, I follow my own Pursuits.

She is holding a lamp in one hand. TARLETON is heard coming in.

          Here's your Uncle now. As for his wanting a
          Son; since I cannot satisfy him, I leave you to
          your Luck.

She exits with the lamp through another door. TARLETON enters, calling.

Tarleton's Word

TARLETON: Jenny! Jenny? … Tom.

TOM: Sir.

TARLETON: When did you come?

TOM: Just now. Jenny met the Coach. And also the
             Colonel's; he's arrived from London. I believe
             she's gone to fetch him down.

TARLETON: So, we're all here. How's your Mother?

TOM: Poor with the Gout, Sir. She saw me off, unable
             to come herself.

TARLETON: I'm sorry. Does she lay off the Drink?

TOM: Her use is moderate; but steady since the Death
             of my Father.

TARLETON: Yes, yes. Well, Tom, good to see you. You've
             spoken to Jenny?

TOM: About?

TARLETON: The Purpose of your Journey.

TOM: That I'm to go aboard the *Jenny*; and hope to
                    quit myself responsibly and to advantage.

TARLETON: I want straight Answers. The Colonel, my
                    Brother, has no Offspring. I have Jenny. Your
                    Mother is a Tarleton. Do you expect Preferment
                    on that Account?

TOM: Our hopes lie in your good Offices, and my
                    own Efforts.

TARLETON: Can you like Jenny?

TOM: She has Spirit; I like her very much.

TARLETON: Yes, her Mother had Spirit, which I liked. She
                    had also Twenty-Thousand a Year, which I
                    liked better.

TOM: That she's my Cousin alarms me. I like her.

TARLETON: Go think, and purge your Scruples on the
                    Passage. I won't pass over my Daughter; I
                    should not wish to disappoint you. There's my
                    Mind.

TARLETON places a hand on TOM's shoulder.

                    And my Word on it.

TOM: You made some mention of this in your Letter.
                    Have you spoken to Jenny?

TARLETON: About?

TOM looks uneasily at TARLETON, who withdraws his hand.
TOM reaches into a pocket, draws and holds out the letter.

                    Burn it. There is only my Word. All the rest

is Tokens – exchange those with Jenny, if you please. My Word, and compliance with it.

JENNY enters and sees them. TOM folds away the letter hurriedly into his pocket. TARLETON puts off his outer coat.

JENNY: Sir, the Colonel has retired. However, I do not think he will sleep.

TARLETON: How so?

JENNY: He is Nervous, agitated. What with the Uncertainty – himself up for re-election – he cannot quite reconcile himself to an honest Fatigue.

TARLETON: I have secured his Seat. As soon as the Count's over he can go back to London.

JENNY: He means to inform you, so long as he's the Member he'll ride out any Clamour for an Abolition – now that this Business looks to come up before the House. But, with so many … irregulars … being elected these Days …

TARLETON: His Seat is safe.

JENNY: Of course, with the young Mr Pitt using Reform, making an Argument of Abolition, to carry a new Government …

TARLETON: Governments fold these Days faster than they stab each other in the Back. Tell him not to worry. Or better – go up and see him comfortable. I'll join him presently.

JENNY goes. TARLETON stony-faced. TOM waits for him to speak.

Pitt might get in. He might take Power.

TOM: He's Young?

TARLETON: And you? Power ages a Man; if you want it

enough, you pay. Pitt will do, sell, anything for Power.

TOM: But an Abolition? On what Grounds could he abolish Trade?

TARLETON: There is an Establishment, Tom. It's Whig, we're part of it. Our family is part of it. Our Business is the life Blood of Whig political Power. Pitt wants to break that Power – or at least, make enough of a Dent in it to accommodate himself.

TOM: His Father was Prime Minister. Perhaps he looks only to Inherit?

TARLETON: Pitt the Younger is not his Father. He wants not only to inherit, but to Change. If he wins the Election, he'll break up the very Ground of Power in the Country.

TOM: Is it possible?

TARLETON unrolls a large map across a table, setting lamps on top to hold it.

TARLETON: Europe, Africa, the Americas – the Continents. Between them, the Western ocean, the Atlantick. Anything that moves must be shipped. That's our Business. Now, point to Britain.

TOM, perplexed, points.

No – not an Island. Britain is here, and here, and here and here. *(Points around the Atlantic)* It is Manufacture, and Sugar; and Slaves, and Tobacco, and Lungs. A protected Market, spanning the Continents. A charmed Circle of Profit. British flags. British Ships. British Guns. Everything we do is protected and subsidised by our Grip on Government. Anything which breaks that is an attack on the Jugular. Pitt knows it. He'll have us by the Throat.

TARLETON rolls up the map, and holds it out to TOM.

> A Token. Pitt has the Power to pull apart the World; We, the Power to make it hold.

TOM takes it; TARLETON doesn't let go.

> Go consider that on the Voyage.

JENNY enters. TARLETON releases the map, to TOM.

JENNY: Do I disturb you? *(To TARLETON)* The Colonel is waiting. He fears the Gout has fixed him to his Chair.

TARLETON: I leave you to yourselves. *(To TOM)* In the Morning.

TARLETON goes.

TOM: Were you listening?

JENNY: To what?

TOM doesn't respond. JENNY walks over, takes and unrolls the map, and, her questioning glance unanswered, begins to pull it apart, laughing. TOM, appalled, takes hold of her arms to stop her. They pause, looking.

JENNY: I want to dance.

TOM: What?

JENNY: We can slip out, now!

She unbuttons the top of his shirt and leans forward to kiss his breast-bone. She leads him off.

> You have no Idea how Liverpool works. You have no Idea how to dance. Until you eat the Indian Opium. Swallow your fear of the Ocean.

SCENE FOUR

Jake's Jig – The Night Watch

Thunder. The sounds of an Irish jig.
JAKE lurks alone at watch on the wet street by the light of an inn door.
JENNY and TOM pass by drunkenly, TOM in a daze, threading the streets.
JAKE watches them go inside.
*He dances the jig, capturing the stagger of a Drunk Man with the aggression of
an Assault.*
The BOSUN comes to the door, watches – nods to JAKE and goes back in.
JAKE pipes a signal on a whistle, gets an answering whistle, and follows in.

Paddy West's House

Inside, the FIDDLER and NEGER SHANTYMAN play a jig.

NEGER SHANTYMAN:

> The Captain likes Whisky and the Devil likes Rum,
> But the Shantyman he can't get none,
> An' when the Cocks begin to crow,
> It's time for him to roll and go!

>> Whisky O, Johnny O! Boys,
>> Rise me up from down below!
>> Whisky O, Johnny O! Boys!
>> Rise me up from down below!

>> I tell you, Boys, in Hell it's hot,
>> You don't get Whisky there on knock;
>> Whisky got me into Debt,

An' the Devil got the Dregs for the Dock-side Press!

> *Whisky O, Johnny O! Boys,*
> *Rise me up from down below!*
> *Whisky O, Johnny O! Boys!*
> *Rise me up from down below!*

The BOSUN stands whispering with JAKE at the bar.
JENNY dances with TOM, dazed and dishevelled – a dance of avoiding his clutches.
The BOSUN follows them over to a corner, where TOM falls in a heap.

BOSUN: I went to Gaol for you.

JENNY looks up and freezes.

                    Remember?

JENNY: You weren't so Ugly.

BOSUN: Gaol's a great Leveller. *(Smiles)* A Rope-Burn
                    would do as worse. I've seen it. A Man stops
                    looking, the Wind shifts, before he knows it,
                    rips his face off. Who's your friend?

JENNY: He's off to Sea – try his Luck where yours ran
                    out. Tom, meet someone's Corpse.

BOSUN: *(To TOM)* Put to Sea with this Girl, Boy, your
                    Feet won't touch the Ground – she'll drag
                    you down. The smell, those looks, the feel, an
                    illusion, don't believe them, soft words, smiles –
                    and all the while she's a Fire-Ship sent to tempt
                    you – with her Father's Money – to put you out
                    of your own Boat. She'll Snare you in Debt –
                    and hold you steady while you Drown.

JENNY: What brings you back to life?

BOSUN: Out on sufferance – to pay my Debt.

JENNY: To your own Ugly Ambition.

BOSUN: To your Bed.

JENNY: Did I run your Ship? Share your Profit?
                      Contract your Debt? You couldn't afford me.

BOSUN: *(Shrugs)* The Worm turns with the Tide. The
                      Sea, now, swallows anything you throw at it:
                      Ships, Rage, Money ... Men. *(Looks at TOM)*
                      They're looking for Crews, he's looking to
                      embark. By the looks of it, staring Disaster in
                      the face.

JENNY: You can't have him.

BOSUN: Got to show Debt, that's all. And it's his
                      Month's Wages, in advance, split down the
                      middle. Share, at least, that with me.

JENNY tries to shake TOM awake. He stirs.

JENNY: Tom ... Time to go.

BOSUN: *(To TOM)* You'd like a Scotch Drink, wouldn't
                      you? Yes, see –

*The BOSUN goes over to the bar to collect a bottle and some glasses. He nods to
JAKE, who turns and leaves.*

JENNY: *(To TOM)* We're going ... Tom ... Tom!

*TOM rouses from his stupor and blinks. The BOSUN returns. He pulls
TOM's arm away from JENNY.*

BOSUN: You just got here.

He pours.

                      (To TOM) Get that down you. Ever put to Sea
                      before?

He makes TOM drink, and pours another.

TOM: Oh, I think that's –

JENNY: That's enough.

BOSUN: They're looking for Backs like yours. You get
                     your Name down quick as you can sign. Had
                     any Experience?

He forces another.

TOM: Umm ...

BOSUN: You'll need more than a Woman, or a Whisky,
                     for a cold Nor'-Wester.

TOM: First Time ... *(Drinks)* Eh, Jenny?

BOSUN: Jenny? Before I'm finished, Madam, I'll have my
                     Dog swear him an Able Seaman. Clear the
                     Decks!

*The BOSUN pushes back the chairs, and lays hold of a wooden pole, a short
piece of canvas and a rope.*

                     Up, Boy! All Hands for'ard!

*The BOSUN pulls TOM sluggishly up onto a chair, TOM clutching on to one
end of the pole.*

JENNY: Tom, no!

*The BOSUN thrusts her back behind him. He steadies the pole, and with his
other arm draws back the rope like a whip. JENNY grabs the rope to stop him
using it.*

BOSUN: You're off. It's blowing a Gale, and a running
                     Sea! What to do? Stow your Main-Royals, of
                     course!

*The BOSUN lets go the pole into TOM's hands. He swings the canvas over the
horizontal yard-arm of TOM's pole like a sail. TOM, off balance, wobbles on
the perch of his chair, about to fall.*

                     Can't furl your Main-Royals?

The BOSUN pulls the rope; JENNY refuses to let it go. They hold it taut.

> *(To JENNY)* What's he worth more than me? *(To TOM)* Right, Lad! Off to South'ard! Here's the Line, over you go!

The BOSUN jerks the taut rope across the back of TOM's legs. TOM gives way at the knees, tumbling from his perch. He lies on the floor.

> Now if they ask you ever been to Sea, you can say you've crossed the Line!

JENNY drops the rope, fetches a pail of dirty water and slews it over TOM. He coughs and retches.

> Man overboard! Clew up your Fore-Top-Ga'nts'ls, Boys, we're taking in the Sea!

JENNY bends over him, her back to the BOSUN. The BOSUN considers her behind.

> Put up your canvas Breeches and give the Boy a rest; Just think of the cold Nor'-Wester that he had in Paddy West's.

The BOSUN takes out a knife. He raises it, and stabs down the blade on the edge of the table – the horn handle upward.

> And now the only thing to do before you sign away – You've crossed the Line and stowed the Jib and been soaked with spray – Is to step around the Table on which there is a Horn …

The BOSUN lifts JENNY bodily from behind and swings her over the horn of the knife by way of demonstration.

> And you can say you've rounded it ten times since you were Born!

The BOSUN holds JENNY tight by the waist; she struggles.
CAPTAIN KNOX and JAKE enter, joined by onlookers in the bar as a GANG – they all carry weapons. The BOSUN releases JENNY and crosses to KNOX. He points to TOM, sprawled on the floor.

That's him.

KNOX walks over and picks up the whisky bottle. He sniffs it, then up-ends and pours its contents out onto the floor.

KNOX: Who'll pay?

JAKE descends on TOM, rifling his pockets and scattering the contents onto the floor – including Tarleton's letter. TOM curls into a foetal position.

JAKE: The Wages of Sin, Is out to Sea before you know.
                         (To KNOX) He has no Money to salvage him.

KNOX gestures to the GANG.

KNOX: Take him quickly!

They pull TOM to his feet. TOM looks into JAKE's face.

TOM: Who are you?

JAKE: I am you –
                         Drowned and splintered,
                         Prone on the Wreck of Adam.
                         The breathing Damage after Storms –
                         The Light and the Wind
                         Listing to your wrack,
                         Where the Sea breaks
                         And the godless Blast lapses into Rage.
                         I am the dark Energy of Creation
                         Dividing you from God –
                         The incomplete, dark Spaces
                         Where He lifted His Face
                         Dripping from the Waters,
                         And divided Himself from the Sea.
                         I am your black Reflection in the Waters –
                         Your Thoughts
                         Lost in long Coils of the Atlantic,
                         Sighing and Hissing.

JAKE lifts TOM onto his shoulders.

                       The Black Angel of Loss –

JENNY flings out a handful of coins, scattered to the floor.

JENNY: He can pay!

BOSUN: What's he to you?

JENNY: I owe you Nothing! Let him go.

JAKE looks to KNOX.
KNOX shakes his head, forbidding him to pick up the coins.
JAKE throws TOM off.

KNOX: *(To the BOSUN)* We won't go empty-handed.
                         Who ordered Drink?

JAKE glances at the BOSUN, and moves away. The BOSUN, eyes fixed
on KNOX, edges toward the knife on the table. KNOX levels a pistol at the
BOSUN's head. The BOSUN looks at JENNY, picks up a glass of whisky and
drinks.

BOSUN:
                'O, Captain, Captain, tell me true,
            Will you tell me where you get your Crew?'
               'I get my Crew from Liverpool,
            And I fetch 'em Drunk from a Girl like you!'
                    Whisky O, Johnny – O!

A groan from the BOSUN as JAKE leaps on his back.
He goes, ushered out through the door by KNOX and the GANG.
JENNY kneels by TOM, embracing him in her shock.

TOM: … the Black Angel …

JENNY: It's the Opium. Dragons flying by you in the
                         Night, but they won't hurt.

She looks about, and begins retrieving his things, strewn on the floor. She finds
her father's letter, opens and reads it. Her expression changes to fury.

JENNY: *(Reads)* 'To take Charge … of my Holdings …
                         in the West India Islands … thereafter … if
                         agreeable to you … Jenny is of an Age …'
                         (Again) 'Jenny is of an Age … wilful … as yet

honest … for you to take her in Hand … In
Hopes to see you established … Your Uncle,
John Tarleton.'

*JENNY glances darkly at TOM. She returns the letter and other things to his
pockets. She fetches the Bosun's glass of whisky, raises and downs it.*

(To TOM) To our Love, Cousin. There's no Man
in the World I'd trust – whose Bones the Ocean
doesn't cradle in her Arms.

She goes.
*The NEGER SHANTYMAN re-enters and clears up, pocketing the scattered
coins.*

NEGER SHANTYMAN: Time for you to roll and go …

He drags TOM out to the street.

SCENE FIVE

<u>The Ground Swell</u>

WILBERFORCE and FOX along the late night corridors of Parliament, FOX waving armfuls of petition papers.

FOX: It's ours! Slavery is the Agenda!

WILBERFORCE: I do not know Semaphore, Mr Fox. Stop waving your Arms.

FOX: We've won! The Tide high for Abolition – Petitions flooding in!

WILBERFORCE: Slight Correction – *Pitt* has won the Election. These are just Petitions. You run up your Flags too soon.

FOX: The Country's behind us! We have a Ground Swell of support for abolishing Slavery!

WILBERFORCE: The Abolition of the *Trade* – in Slaves. Yes, we have a Number of Friends.

FOX: We have Support, Sir!

WILBERFORCE: *(Absentmindedly taking a paper)* It worries me the Petitions are all identically worded. The Opposition will have wind of us. I suppose the thing to do is use them to table a single Motion before the House.

FOX: Table a Motion? We have a Mandate!

WILBERFORCE: Or perhaps it might, on balance, be better to put
                    it through a Committee stage: examine into
                    Evidence for action against the Trade.

FOX: We have a Mandate for abolishing an Evil, and
                    you talk of Evidence?

WILBERFORCE: This is a Parliamentary Democracy. Let us not
                    stifle Debate.

FOX: The Petitions –

WILBERFORCE: Do you know, in the American States, to "table
                    a Motion" is no longer to run up a Debate, but
                    to throw it out? You are fortunate to belong to
                    the British system.

PITT enters, catching the last of the exchange. They see him.

WILBERFORCE: *(To PITT)* Mr Pitt. Congratulations.

PITT: Well done, Gentlemen. *(To FOX)* Welcome to
                    the House, Mr Fox. Unfortunately, I have a
                    Rival of that name already here. I hope I won't
                    confuse you. *(To both)* So, what can I do for you?

WILBERFORCE: My young Friend wishes to urge your Attention
                    to the matter of that pernicious Trade in Slaves.

PITT: *(To FOX)* What is your Interest in the matter?

FOX: To make it yours.

PITT: Why should it be mine?

FOX: Because I mean to see it Abolished.

PITT looks from FOX to WILBERFORCE, and back to FOX.

PITT: Yes, I believe you could make a Nuisance of
                    yourself. Slavery – Millions bred, bought,

transported, killed. And at what Cost – in Men and Capital. What Waste of Human Potential. But with the Loss of the American Colonies – to which my Father never was entirely reconciled – goes the Problem: What to do with another Continent of Black Men? It is a Demographic Enormity, but are we the Atlas to set it right? Have you a good Pair of Shoulders?

FOX, astonished, looks to WILBERFORCE, then back to PITT.

FOX: No, Mr Pitt, they do not carry the Burden of State. I imagine myself a Slave – of too young an Age to conceive of Death. And yet I am dead to the World, chained in place, without Benefit of Father, Friend, Lover or any Language of the Heart. I am chained below in that Ship of State anchored somewhere off the known, un-fettered World, my Language lying to rust, a Poem lost each Day from my Mouth. I am not an Atlas. I am the World's Pulse.

WILBERFORCE coughs into an embarrassed silence.

PITT: A spokesman. Wilberforce, you may steer it through the House, with my support. It is to the East, for trade to India we must turn our Guns. America is a lost Cause. *(Bowing)* Mr Fox.

PITT goes; FOX turns, shocked, to WILBERFORCE, who coughs again.

FOX: And if I refuse – on my Conscience – to join this Place?

WILBERFORCE: Then you would have no Voice. You would not be heard.

WILBERFORCE goes.
FOX slumps and drops petition papers to the floor.
He kneels to pick them up; the NEGER SHANTYMAN enters and joins him.
Taking one from his hand, FOX looks up into the face.

FOX: Believe me, if you could read – what is now being unwritten.

Leaving some scattered, FOX goes.

NEGER SHANTYMAN: *(Reads as he goes)* "Petition of the People called Quakers ... having solemnly considered the state of the enslaved negroes ... to lay the suffering ... before you." *(Reads from another)* "Petition of the inhabitants of Bridgwater, Somerset ..." *(Another)* "Petition from the parishioners of West Calder, West Lothian ..." *(Another)* "Petition from the inhabitants of Manchester ... in support of the Abolition ..." *(Another)* "Petition from Manufacturers and Merchants of Manchester against the Abolition Bill ... [Lifts an eyebrow] For, and Against."

He goes.

SCENE SIX

The Pier-Head

CAPTAIN KNOX and TOM about to board the Blackamoor Jenny.

KNOX: Your Uncle, Mr Tarleton, insisted you come. It
          was not my Wish; I make no Secret of that.
          I trust you will give me no Cause to be
          displeased with your Conduct. I am absolute
          Master of my Ship.

TOM: I am here to learn, Sir.

JENNY steps out behind them, and waves.

JENNY: Tom?

KNOX looks at TOM.

KNOX: It's late not to have completed your Farewells.
          The Tide won't wait. And the Pier-Head is a
          public Place.

TOM lowers his head before KNOX, who looks at JENNY.

          In every Port there are Women fluttering
          handkerchiefs and petticoats. Personally, I
          dislike the estranged Semaphore of Parting.

KNOX goes. TOM turns back to JENNY.

JENNY: Did you forget me?

TOM: It was early. Your Father thought not to wake you.

JENNY: All Night I couldn't sleep. I watched you leave from the Window, and followed. See?

JENNY parts her coat. Beneath is her unbuttoned night-dress. TOM looks to the ship.

TOM: I must go.

JENNY: Do you miss me? Or do I Dream?

TOM: There is Fog enough in my mind; I must remain Awake.

JENNY: *(Takes his hand to place on her breast)* And feel Nothing for me?

TOM: I feel – I cannot afford to be Troubled.

JENNY: I am Trouble? What else must you keep Locked in your Chest?

TOM: My own Heart, of course – I cannot Doubt; I have a Fortune to make. I cannot see into the Depth of yours.

The ship's bell begins to ring. TOM turns to go.

Four, five Months, I'll be Home. Let your Hair grow long. I'll have a Ribbon for it when I come.

JENNY: *(Taking him by the Sleeve)* To tie up your Affairs?

TOM steps forward and kisses her.

TOM: You play the Whore; I'll play Cruel, and Fearless. And no one will know, what Bad children we are; hiding from one another. Don't – Don't fight me –: I wouldn't Steal your Fortune, or Force your Affection. But Fortune has pushed us together. We must weather it,

Jenny. Only know: I will be in Command. It is my Duty. *(Bows)* Madam.

TOM goes.

JENNY: Goodbye, Cousin.

The BOSUN, chained in leg irons, comes up behind JENNY, and watches with her.

Keep your Red Ribbons.

BOSUN: To snarl up your bonny black Hair?

JENNY spins round.

JENNY: Keep back your Ribbons for the Judge.

BOSUN: The Black Wig? Murther? What can the Matter be?

JENNY: Men were born Deceivers. But I think ahead …

Indicating his full attention, JENNY throws down the Key to unlock his irons. Furtive, he immediately sits to unlocking his feet, and his thought.

You are not Shackled to your Debt. You go freely aboard the *Jenny* – as Bosun.

BOSUN: *(Holding in question the irons)* Who broke the Chain?

JENNY: It is your Merit. You belong to this Business. *(Glances to the ship)* Were he not to come back … Who knows?

BOSUN: *(Standing)* You'd owe me. But then, you already do.

JENNY reaches out to touch his face. He recoils. She touches his chest.

JENNY: All your Debts paid in full.

BOSUN: Why a Man dies, who knows? But he must know why he lives.

The BOSUN catches hold of her wrist as she pulls away.

JENNY: A Woman, on both Counts. And there's Money in it.

BOSUN: Always is. Part Passion, part Fraud. But it's never enough.

The BOSUN reaches to the nape of her neck, and yanks off her necklace. JENNY tries to snatch it back. He pushes her off, opening the locket and looking at it.

Engraved. To you. Who gave you this?

JENNY doesn't respond; he pockets the necklace.

That's my Insurance. I must have something to plead to the Judge. This Time it's a Gentleman mounting your Scaffold; you'll Hang for that.

JENNY: It's both our Necks.

BOSUN: It is now. We can Hang together; either way I get to clamber on your Bones.

JENNY: You'd climb that Ladder to my Bed? Have a Care.

BOSUN: *(Smiles)* Wait on the Tide. Someone will come back for you.

The BOSUN throws down his leg irons at her feet, pockets the Key and goes. JENNY stands alone on the Pier-Head.

JENNY: My Heart is mine. Not any Man's to strike a bell …

The Shanty Chorus

NEGER SHANTYMAN (off):

> One Man to strike the Bell
> High O! Come haul her over!
> Two Men to man the Wheel
> Wind-ho! Why don't you blow?
> Three Men to Gallant-Braces
> High O! Come haul her over!
> Four Men to board the Tack
> Wind-ho! Why don't you blow?

The deck of the Blackamoor Jenny. CAPTAIN KNOX and TOM enter on the fo'c'sle – a raised area. The BOSUN passes beneath.

BOSUN: Captain!

KNOX: Is the Pilot aboard?

BOSUN: Aye, Sir.

KNOX: Then carry on, Bosun, move her off.

The BOSUN blows his whistle and goes.

SHANTY CHORUS (off):

> Five Men to heave the Lead
> High O! Come haul her over!
> Six Men to furl T'g'ns'ls
> Wind-ho! Why don't you blow?
> Seven Men to Gallant-Braces
> High O! Come haul her over!
> Eight Men to just One Girl
> Wind-ho! Come haul her over!

KNOX: Who was that on the Pier-Head?

TOM: No one. I'm whole-hearted for the Voyage.

KNOX: Just as well.

BOSUN *(Off)*:   Strike up there!

SHANTY CHORUS *(off)*:

> *The Chain's up and down the Bosun did say,*
> *Away for Guinea!*
> *It's up to the Hawse-Pipe, the Anchor's aweigh*
> *An' it's goodbye to Liverpool Town!*

> *So away, my Love, away*
> *Bound for Guinea!*
> *It's Farewell to Maggie, it's farewell to Sue,*
> *An' you on the Pier-Head it's farewell to you*
> *An' it's goodbye to Liverpool Town!*

KNOX: Carry on.

KNOX goes; TOM stands looking out.
The harbour bell rings; JENNY turns and leaves from the pier-head.

NEGER SHANTYMAN *(off)*:

> *A Ship went sailing over the Bar,*
> *Bound for Guinea!*
> *They've pointed her Bow to the Southern Star*
> *An' it's goodbye to Liverpool Town!*

Another bell, for the Committee. The two bells sway back and forth. The harbour bell finally recedes – recurring as a sound throughout the next scene, rising towards the end as the sense of a storm threatens to break in on the Committee.

SHANTY CHORUS *(off)*:

> *So away, my Boys, away!*
> *Black'moor Jenny!*
> *Scrub her, and Tar her, and dress up her Sails,*
> *'Fore she heads into those black Biscay Gales*
> *An' it's goodbye to Liverpool Town!*

The Select Committee: Storms, Wrecks and Losses

WILBERFORCE, FOX and BALZIEL enter. The petitions are read after the overlapping pattern of a round. TOM remains visible throughout.

PETITION 1:	Petition, 8th February, 1792, that: the African Slave Trade is contrary to the Principles of Justice, Humanity and Religion, and ought to be abolished.
PETITION 2:	Petition, 10th February, that: the Merchants of Liverpool have trusted and embarked the whole of their Fortunes and Families in the Slave Trade.
PETITION 3:	15th February, that: founded on the Oppression of one Part of Mankind, no System can be beneficial to another.
PETITION 4:	22nd February, that: the Ships of the African Trade have suffered Storms, Wrecks and Losses for the Wealth of the Nation, and have floated in Time of War for its Defence.
PETITION 5:	27th February, that: Dangers can never justify a Crime, nor atone for its Guilt.
WIBERFORCE:	Said Petitions were ordered to be read, and to lie upon the table of this Committee of the House.

WILBERFORCE places the petitions down on a table resembling the dispatch-box in the House, along the central aisle of the Ship. FOX stands to ask questions; WILBERFORCE sits beside him. CAPTAIN BALZIEL stands opposite.

FOX:	Your name?
BALZIEL:	Captain Archibald Balziel.
FOX:	You are a Bristol Merchant?

BALZIEL: I am.

FOX: Can you form any Estimate of the Profits of the
                  African Slave Trade to the Merchants of Bristol?

BALZIEL: It's a precarious Trade. Sometimes Profit's
                  good, sometimes not so.

FOX: In what Ship was it you lost so many of the
                  Crew?

BALZIEL: What?

FOX: What was the name of Ship you commanded in
                  the Year 1786?

BALZIEL: The *Ruby*.

FOX: What was the Number of the Crew?

BALZIEL: I cannot remember exactly – thirty-six or thirty-
                  seven.

FOX: What Number died?

BALZIEL: Five, or six, or seven – to the best of my
                  Remembrance.

FOX: Not fifteen, or sixteen …?

BALZIEL: I am pretty confident not so many died.

FOX: In the Years 1780, '81, '85 and '86, you
                  commanded Ships to the Coast of Africa
                  to purchase Slaves. Were those Voyages
                  profitable?

BALZIEL: I believe they were all Voyages that a certain
                  Profit attended.

FOX: Excluding Slaves – that last Voyage alone was
                  attended by some five, or six, or seven fellow
                  human Deaths, according to your Estimation.
                  What was it worth?

BALZIEL doesn't respond. WILBERFORCE leans over to FOX.

WIBERFORCE: Facts, Mr Fox. As far as possible.

FOX: *(To BALZIEL)* Had you a Ship called *The Brothers?*

BALZIEL doesn't respond.

                    The Brothers?

BALZIEL: Yes.

FOX: That you commanded in the Year 1787 in the African Trade?

BALZIEL: I did. And made a very fatal Voyage. I do not want to conceal anything from this Committee.

FOX: How many of her Crew did you lose?

BALZIEL: A full Third of my Ship's Company – to the best of my Remembrance– not having the Account about me.

FOX: You did not lose above Half your Ship's Company?

BALZIEL: I cannot be sure. I didn't think to bring the Account with me. I have been twenty years in the trade. Only a Boy when I entered it. And very little deserving to have been called before this Committee. I was not prepared for – The Voyages I undertook were Lawful, and in Good Faith.

FOX: A full Half?

BALZIEL: I cannot say exactly. I had eight drowned by Accident at one Time; two or three at another … Below Biscay there is no trusting what the Sea will do.

FOX:	As Captain, you are to account for that Mortality?
BALZIEL:	I treated the Crew as befits the Sinews of a Trading Vessel. When I see a good, healthy Fellow that I can put a Trust in in a Gale of Wind, I always give him a Guinea or two more than a Man I cannot confide in.
FOX:	Does ill-treatment of the Crews account for the Mortality aboard these Ships?
BALZIEL:	You will find the Captains of Guineamen are tolerable on their first sailing. Cruelty begins to show itself only on Arrival upon the Coast. After they have been there a little Time, it has no Bounds. That was not my way. Yet it is I who am called.
FOX:	What is the Dead List?
BALZIEL:	An Account of Seamen who have died at Sea, for the forwarding any Wages to their Dependents.
FOX:	From the List of your Ship, *The Brothers*, twenty-five Seamen lost their lives.
BALZIEL:	So many?
FOX:	Among the Slaves, how many died?
BALZIEL:	Of 300 and upwards that we sailed with ... I was detained a six-Month upon the Coast at Benin – with the Small Pox, then the Yellow Fever, Dysentery ...
FOX:	How many died?

BALZIEL doesn't respond.

Of the 300 and upward you sailed with, how many?

BALZIEL: A Third?

A moment.

WILBERFORCE: A Third? ... God rest their 100 Souls.

BALZIEL doesn't respond. The committee bell, and the harbour bell as before. FOX turns and leaves. WILBERFORCE crosses to BALZIEL, takes him by the arm and leads him away.

BALZIEL: A six-Month – Provisions scarce – few Slaves to
                           be had from the Factories – exposed to all
                           Weathers – Rains, the miasma of the Smokes –
                           reckoned very unwholesome – no Relief – the
                           Slaves rotting – the Crew rotting – Come in
                           contact – all we could do was kill each other –
                           so many dying – It was all my Power to stay
                           alive ...

They go.

SCENE SEVEN

The Land Wind

TOM on deck, the BOSUN enters with a Spy-Glass, hauling the CABIN-BOY by the collar.

BOSUN: Unreeve that Tackle! Turn her about! You there! Clew in the Courses to Wind-ward, and run her! *(To the CABIN-BOY)* One Hand to the Cross-Trees, one to the Spy-Glass! Shout what you see!

He shoves the CABIN-BOY off.

TOM: Why are we turning about?

BOSUN: Hold to your Stomach. We're lurching to a Land-Wind. Keep to the After-Guard.

The BOSUN goes.

TOM: Land?

SHANTY CHORUS *(off)*:

> *Haul all together, aye, yeo!*
> *To the Cat-Head!*
> *Haul for good Weather, aye, yeo!*
> *She's heavy as Lead!*
> *For worse or for better, aye, yeo!*
> *Raise from the Dead!*
> *Oh, hauley, aye, yeo!*
> *Haul, the Man said!*

SURGEON *(Off)*:   Who's turning us about?

The SURGEON enters.
The CABIN-BOY calls from above.

CABIN-BOY *(Off)*:   Land!

The SURGEON looks up.

SURGEON: Who sent that Boy aloft? Come down before he
                     breaks his neck!

TOM: *(Points)* The Edge of Africa!

The SURGEON looks to where TOM points.

SURGEON: That's the dark Edge of a Land-Wind. You
                     won't get any closer till it drops.

TOM: It's Land. That smell – I can feel – the heat!

SURGEON: You can smell your Stomach, turning about. It's
                     the Wind. Who sent that Boy up into it? *(Shouts)*
                     Bosun!

The BOSUN enters.

                     Who gave the Order to go?

BOSUN: We're beating to the Coast.

SURGEON: The only thing reaching into this Wind's a
                     Bogful of Spittle – and that's blinding my Eye!
                     Go wake the Captain. Tell him we're caught
                     in a Land-Wind. If he wants, we'll go – but we
                     might as well drop Anchor in his sleep and
                     wait. *(Looks up)* And bring down that Boy!

The BOSUN goes.

                     There's a bad Crack in that Man's Eye.

TOM: Sir?

SURGEON:	You get a better Face on a Cadaver. Weather's the Soul of this Trade. Years in it can shrivel a man.
TOM:	Is that a Medical Opinion?
SURGEON:	A Superstition.
TOM:	Then does it belong on this Ship?

TOM and the SURGEON look hard at each other – steadying themselves on the moving ship.

SURGEON:	Do I belong? A Man born when that Jib-boom was a sapling Trunk in Epping? Qualified by the Surgeons of Surgeon's Hall as capable of serving aboard any of His Majesty's Ships of any Rate? Six Months' Grog on Credit can uproot a Man. So here I am.
TOM:	That Man's here for Debt – he weathers it. You've to bend if you're to get an Edge of Profit under Sails.
SURGEON:	*(Points)* Wind's the Guardian of this Coast. I'm the Surgeon; and I know there's a Toll on entering there. A Dead Man's Guinea – each one stamped with a Stranger's Face.

The BOSUN passes along the deck, and exits shouting.

BOSUN:	Belay all! Furl her up! Hands to the Capstan and drop Anchor!
SURGEON:	See you at Breakfast.

The SURGEON goes.
The CABIN-BOY enters, shivering. TOM stops him.

TOM:	What did you see?
CABIN-BOY:	Land, Sir.

TOM: Clearly?

CABIN-BOY: It was a blowing Wind, Sir, up on the Cross-
                        Trees. Couldn't stop long, in case I took a
                        Fall. It was … or, I couldn't be sure … a black
                        Thunder-Squall. I'm to go before the Mast, Sir,
                        if I'm to have any Breakfast.

TOM: A Squall?

CABIN-BOY: I saw the Sails tossed under me. It was like
                        riding an Angel, Sir, in the Sails, moving fast on
                        the Water – a Squall of Thunder, or Land rising
                        to meet me. Black as a Devil's wing.

TOM looks at the CABIN-BOY, who stands shivering.

TOM: How old are you?

CABIN-BOY: Fourteen.

TOM: So old?

The CABIN-BOY lowers his head.

                        Been to Africa before?

CABIN-BOY: No, Sir.

TOM: Frightened?

CABIN-BOY: No, Sir. Hungry.

The BOSUN shouts off-stage.

BOSUN *(Off)*:   Hang, you Sons of Whores! Hang Heavy! Stow
                        Hammocks, and go before the Mast.

The CABIN-BOY, fear in his eye, looks anxiously up at TOM.

TOM: Go.

The BOSUN enters and sees them. The CABIN-BOY retreats and goes.

BOSUN:	Pity to see his white Fingers so besmirched with Pitch and Tar. Looks just like a Girl.

TOM stares after the CABIN-BOY.

	Will you go for Breakfast?
TOM:	Not hungry.
BOSUN:	The Food. Thought you should know. The feeling is it's Strange. They're your Rations.
TOM:	Musty meat, weevily Biscuit – what's the Matter?
BOSUN:	Food's an Anchor, and it's my Job to weigh it up. If Men don't eat, and this Wind don't abate ...
TOM:	What's wrong with it?
BOSUN:	The Salt-Pork. Jack Strahan got a Sow's Under-Belly – Nipple you could suck on thick as my Finger.
TOM:	They'll get an Appetite for it.
BOSUN:	*(Shrugs)* If they can't get what they left at Home.

The BOSUN goes.
The CABIN-BOY re-enters, shivering, and crouches down with a plate of food.
TOM watches him eat.
The NEGER SHANTYMAN enters unobtrusively, crouching down with a cup of rum to watch.

The Shape Change

NEGER SHANTYMAN:

> *She put herself in Sailor's Clothes*
> *And signed herself aboard a Ship,*
> *Where she performed a Seaman's Chores*
> *Of Miracle and Seamanship.*

Her Lips were Rubies rubbed with Salt
The Salt was in her sloe-black Hair,
The Sweat stood out upon her Shirt,
With Nipples thick as my Finger.

She went aloft to furl a Sail
With one Man who found out her Sex,
The Wind Blew open her Waistcoat
And exposed a milk-white Breast.

A Pact of Silence she has made
To keep the Secret from the Crew –
'Although I'm neither Man nor Maid
For silence I'll be kind to you.'

JAKE enters, and sees TOM staring at the CABIN-BOY, who looks up,
glancing through TOM with frightened eyes, at JAKE.

TOM: *(Turning to JAKE)* What?

JAKE: You eat with your Eyes? *(Points at the CABIN-
                       BOY)* What's wrong?

CABIN-BOY: Got the Shivers.

TOM: *(To JAKE)* He went aloft. Got soaked to the
                       Skin. The Wind's gone through him.

JAKE: *(Advancing on the CABIN-BOY)* This Wind
                       sees you, sifts you, shapes you – holds you
                       from the Coast.

TOM: What the –

The CABIN-BOY backs away in fear, blocked by the BOSUN, who re-enters.

BOSUN: *(To JAKE)* Abate, Blackee. *(To the CABIN-BOY)*
                       The Men want to know what you're made of –
                       Flesh or Fish?

JAKE: *(To TOM)* Whale-meat, or Wind …

CABIN-BOY: I'm not! Don't say it –

TOM: For God's Sake!

TOM tries to intervene; JAKE blocks and silences him with a finger to the lips. The BOSUN corners the CABIN-BOY with an edge of menace, seizes hold him and beckons to the CREW, appearing one by one.

BOSUN: Flesh – or Fish?

The CREW hold the CABIN-BOY with the BOSUN, stripping off his shoes and stockings, then swinging as if to throw him overboard.

CREW: *Salt Pork, Salt Pork, we'd have you know*
                  That to the Galley you must go.

                  The Cook without a Sign of Grief
                  Will boil you down and call you Beef.

                  And we poor Sailors standing near
                  Must eat you though you look so queer

                  We'll tan your Hide and braise your Bones
                  And pack you off to Davy Jones.

                  We'll salt you down for Sailor's use
                  And pick your Bones and suck your Juice.

                  And if you don't believe it's true
                  Look in the Pot, you'll find a Shoe.

                  It's groan you may but go you must
                  To make this Wind blow over us!

CABIN-BOY: Mercy!

TOM steps between them and the side.

TOM: I'm responsible for Provisions here. You'll eat
                  what I give!

BOSUN: Just a bit of fun, Sir. Nothing meant by it. She
                  just crossed the Line.

The CAPTAIN enters, dressing.

CAPTAIN: What's here?

TOM: Nothing, Sir. The Men become light-headed. It's this Wind.

CAPTAIN: Throw your sour Provisions to the Sea, empty the Water-Barrels. I want the Ship lightened. We're going in. *(To the BOSUN)* Man your Stations.

The BOSUN whistles, the CREW disperse.

(To TOM) It's bad practice to pig in among the Sailors. Keep to the After-Guard for your Society.

TOM: It lightens the mood. This Wind's oppressive when –

CAPTAIN: We're going for the Coast, Sir. There's a Grave for them and they know it. When the Yellow Jack gets aboard, killing, I want the Discipline in place to deal with it.

TOM: I was not –

CAPTAIN: Damn it, Man! If you can't get on, get off! I've a Ship to run! Calculate my Costs; I want an Inventory of Stores once you've chucked your Baggage over-Board, and no Qualms from you! We start taking Stores and Slaves on arrival.

TOM: Sir.

CAPTAIN: Carry on.

The CAPTAIN goes.
The CABIN-BOY creeps past barefoot to gather his shoes, glances at TOM and goes.

NEGER SHANTYMAN *(off)*:

> *We sailed away to the White Man's Grave,*
> *An evil Wind made our Top-s'ls shake, and*
> *Blow me, Boys, and blow for ever,*
> *Blow me down in the Black Man's Weather!*
>
> *Here she comes with her rusty Chains on,*
> *Blood in the Scuppers and the Sails gone rotten!*
>
> *(Chorus)*
>
> *Ever wish you was dead and buried?*
> *Yellow Jack's come with his groaning Ferry!*
>
> *(Chorus)*
>
> *Another pull, now, rock and shake her,*
> *Go she must and go we'll make her!*
>
> *(Chorus)*

TOM: Steady on.

Tom goes.

SCENE EIGHT

Jenny and Tarleton:

TARLETON, reading a letter by a lighted window, JENNY enters, interrupting him.

JENNY: News?

TARLETON: What?

JENNY: Tom?

TARLETON, alert, looks up.

TARLETON: Worried?

JENNY: Concerned. He's my Cousin.

TARLETON: So far as I know, he should be leaving the Slave Coast by now; it depends how long they are Detained. To lose him to its Smokes and sickly Rains would grieve me to the Core. But lose this Business of Abolition, would grieve us all.

JENNY: Lose?

TARLETON: Abolition's a Whale – one Flunder of her Tail, we all capsize.

JENNY: News from London.

TARLETON: I've been called to give Evidence before a

	House Committee on the Trade. I leave in the Morning.
JENNY:	What will you say?
TARLETON:	This is Pitt's doing. We must appear to compromise. Suggest some Regulation of the Trade; the Dead hand of Regulation on Shipping. Very unpopular. Offer Bait.
JENNY:	Will they bite?
TARLETON:	I doubt it. But it shifts the Sway of Emotions away from Abolition onto the Complexities of Regulation. Better tangled in those Nets, than bump the Boat proper.
JENNY:	A Ploy? Is that how you do it? Snarl up any Threat to keep it off?

TARLETON frowns.

TARLETON:	I'm protecting your Interests.
JENNY:	Mine, or Tom's?
TARLETON:	Don't press into Politics. It's more than desolate for a Man. How should you weather it?
JENNY:	Alone? May I not go with you to London? Perhaps I can amuse myself in the Pleasure Gardens at Vauxhall?
TARLETON:	You have the run of this House. Attend to that.
JENNY:	With Tom to Africa, you in London, I must stay at Anchor?
TARLETON:	When Tom returns, and so do I, what more is there?
JENNY:	I imagine his return – from Africa, the West India Plantations. Whereas I cannot speak with

any Certainty of London.

TARLETON: There are Worlds you were best sheltered from.

JENNY: Only one hears such Tales … of Life in the Plantations. And to think, my Mother was born there …

TARLETON doesn't respond.

In fact, I heard of a Woman, a Creole, who told her Slave, "Go to the Overseer, give my Service to him, and this Shilling, and tell him to give you 27 Lashes." Is that true? I heard tell of it from a young Officer … when to withhold a Shilling I consider an ample Discipline in the Management of our Servants.

TARLETON: They are not Negroes.

JENNY: Has that some bearing?

TARLETON: Bear in mind, Negroes are naturally Turbulent, and Indolent. They want Exertion when not forced to work. It is necessary to be rigid and severe for them to understand you.

JENNY: I understand Severity. Also, how much Tenderness becomes the care of any mortal Being.

TARLETON: Indulge me.

JENNY: Are not Negroe Women open to wanton Gazes, rough Attacks from the Sailors? Or do their Officers, on Ship, ensure a more becoming Tenderness?

TARLETON: I do not see everything that is done. Neither does Tom. What's more, we earn our Bread by it. Be so perverse, if you will, as to question Negroe Men: they have no Idea of private Property, beyond immediate occupancy. They

take and have done. How then should I, or
Tom, judge a becoming Tenderness?

JENNY: How could you not? Are the Women not
bought and examined as a Horse is in this
Country?

TARLETON: Of course I should look in your Eyes, to see if
you were blind, as I should a Horse in this
Country, if I was to purchase you. And also
question your Limbs.

JENNY: And were there such a Market, in this Country,
to which every Person may promiscuously go
to purchase Male and Female human beings,
would you be there?

TARLETON: Do you live in a Country where there is no
one rich enough to buy another; none so Poor
as not forced to sell Themselves?

JENNY: I have seen my own Freedom openly offered. It
is an Abuse.

TARLETON: Then know I mean to fetch your best Price, and
see you not ill-Used. It's my Duty as a Father.

JENNY: To see me sold? For Fear of losing me?

TARLETON does not respond.

I have heard your Captains say, piping their
Tobacco, that People watch in the long Grass
at Angola, and make Slaves of all who chance
to pass. And that more Slaves are brought
down to the Ships at a Full-Moon than at any
other Time. Is that not strange? Were I to be
estranged in that way, stolen by the Moon into
a derelict Place, by Shadows moving in the
Silvered Grass, my dear Captains piping their
Tobacco – how harsh a Place that World might
seem. So full of losing.

TARLETON rises to go.

> I cannot forever sit at their Knee, hiding from the waiting Ships, my Mother's Death, or yours. Or mine. Better now I know what you feel; you will not always be here to Acquaint me with it. You cannot secrete your Shadows from me: they are in me. Open up, before they rise in me, from the long Grass, and strike you down!

TARLETON: What do you want from me?

JENNY: I will not be passed over.

TARLETON remains still, looking at her; then goes abruptly.

TARLETON: We leave for London in the morning.

JENNY stands alone, looking to the lighted window.

SCENE TEN

The Night Attack

The sound of a bell. TOM enters with a sea service Pistol and a Bloodied cutlass. He shakes the Cutlass from his grasp. It clatters to the deck. JAKE rushes past with a musket and Depth-Lead.

TOM: What's that Bell?

JAKE spins, startled, and sees TOM crouching.

JAKE: A dark Hint
                        Of the last Hours –
                        In the Stinking swamp.

BOSUN *(Off)*:   Keep watch of the Land-Side! They strike an
                        Alarm!

JAKE sees the cutlass, picks it up and looks at it; it drips blood. TOM recoils.

JAKE: A Slave-Bell in the Christian settlement –
                        Crying the Sins of Man – startling
                        Swarms of Mosquitoes from the Blood!

JAKE licks the blade with a thumb and tastes it on his tongue.

                        You've tasted the Sea – It's Salt Work.

JAKE daubs a cross of blood on Tom's forehead with his thumb.

                        You – with your Counting – your Balance-Sheets –
                        Sin in Pound Sterling – The Blood you came for.

CAPTAIN *(Off)*: Take a Cast of the Lead!

JAKE goes to the side and casts the lead, a to-and-fro movement.

What water have you?

JAKE *(Shouts)*: By the Deep, Four! And a half Three! *(To TOM)* All the Oceans in your Mouth Won't clear you. So breathe Air, and admit Nothing!

CAPTAIN *(Off)*: Damn her, won't she move?

The sound of sporadic musket fire. The CAPTAIN enters, barking orders up at the crew.

Shorten sail! Let go the Chain-Cable or she'll run aground! Cut their Boat-Hooks! Prepare to return Fire!

BOSUN *(Off)*: Re-load!

CAPTAIN: *(Seeing TOM)* Tarleton.

The CAPTAIN grabs TOM's Pistol and exits. TOM crouches closer. JAKE secures the lead-chain to a belaying pin and starts to haul in.

TOM: Who's there?

JAKE: The Devil trying to board us – catch and cut our Throats! Up! *(Reaches and thrusts the cutlass back to TOM's hand)* You're Salt-Pork strung in the Beams!

TOM: I'm shot.

JAKE stops, and stares at TOM – who collapses, his hand at his side bloody.

BOSUN *(Off)*: Fire at Will!

A volley of musket-shot. Cries, groans, shouts, curses.

CAPTAIN *(Off)*: She moves! Hands, make Sail! Up! We run with the Wind!

JAKE crouches and reloads his musket. Ramming home the powder and shot with vigorous thrusts, he looks up into the rigging – the sound of a land-wind, the flap of sail, hesitant at first, then faster.

JAKE: Ay!
You took a NEGROE by the Toe to your own
Destruction!
A NEGROE, huge as the dark Stars of the
Southern Cross!
Shackled, crucified!

Look!
Sails flying from Mood to Mood like a Mad
Man
To his own Destruction!

The slack of the lead-chain is taken up with a yank. They both freeze.

Here's Someone howling up for you. The most
Ugly, miserable Specimen of NEGROE ever you
clapped eyes on – I think it's a Fiend!

JAKE shifts, releases the belaying-pin holding the lead-chain, and crouches back down as it rattles away over the side.

If it hollers, *let it go* ...

The BOSUN enters, shouting, with a musket.

BOSUN: *(To JAKE)* You there! To work! Watch for their
Boats!

JAKE: *(To TOM)* Say your Prayers.

A shot. JAKE, his musket loaded, rushes off. The BOSUN stands over TOM and raises the butt of his musket, pushing him down onto his back.

BOSUN: You saw who shot you?

TOM slowly shakes his head.

I've no Use for you.

The SURGEON enters, head bandaged, led by the CABIN-BOY, and stares at the BOSUN. The BOSUN lowers his musket.

SURGEON: *(To the BOSUN)* Dead?

BOSUN: Good as.

SURGEON: He's lost blood.

BOSUN Do what you can, before we pitch the Corpses over-Board.

The BOSUN turns to go.

SURGEON: You'd overthrow your Captain's Credit?

BOSUN: You mend his Pence, Surgeon. I'll shackle his Pound.

The BOSUN goes. The SURGEON kneels to examine TOM's body and compress the wound.

SURGEON: *(To the CABIN-BOY)* Bring me an Oil-Lamp from the Cook-Pit, a Knife, Tongs, Gauzes – and a Piece of Leather. A Bottle of Spirits, too. Be quick!

The CABIN-BOY goes. The SURGEON slaps TOM's face.

Don't sleep.

TOM struggles to rise; the SURGEON holds him down.

Aye, lie still. I'll do what I can. So many Dead they hardly need me now. I'm thrown among the Boys of the Ship; not treated like a Man, nor yet like an honest Boy. The Men so full of obeying and Fearing ... as dangerous Dogs obey and fear their Master.

The CABIN-BOY returns with the SURGEON's things, holding a lighted oil-lamp.

CAPTAIN *(Off)*:   Clear those Corpses!

The SURGEON prepares his things, heating the knife and tongs in the lighted oil-lamp held by the CABIN-BOY.

TOM: *(An effort)* ... You saw?

SURGEON: *(Nods)* We lost one of the Boats, with its Crew of Five. Two more as they attacked the Ship. Some others missing. We must swing with a Skeleton Crew now.

CAPTAIN *(Off)*:   We therefore commit their bodies to the Deep ...

The sound of a splash. Another splash. They listen.

SURGEON: *(A moment)* ... to be turned into Corruption, looking for the Resurrection of the Body when the Sea shall give up her Dead.

The SURGEON pulls a bottle of whisky from his bag and swigs.

(To the CABIN-BOY) Give him that.

The CABIN-BOY sets it to TOM's lips.

This will hurt.

A surgeon's nod. The CABIN-BOY puts a piece of leather between TOM's teeth.

Hold fast!

The CABIN-BOY falls across TOM's legs; the SURGEON kneels across him and wrestles out a bullet with the knife and tongs. TOM arcs his back, then collapses back, silent. The SURGEON acts to stem the bleeding. He holds up a piece of lead between the tongs and looks at it in the light of the oil-lamp.

Intact.

He lets it drop. They release TOM.

CABIN-BOY: Won't he cry out?

SURGEON: For what? Let him have his Black-out.

The SURGEON begins re-placing his tools; picks up the bottle, looks at it, swigs.

                              Lest we forget.

CABIN-BOY: He needs to get out of the Wind.

The BOSUN enters.

BOSUN: Throw a Canvas on him. The Hatch is down. It won't come up till Morning.

The BOSUN reaches into the SURGEON's hand, lifts the bottle and takes a long swig.

                              By Morning, he'll be stiff, and over-Board. *(To the CABIN-BOY)* But we're alive, eh?

The BOSUN swigs again, and thrusts the bottle into the CABIN-BOY'S hand.

                              Something to break your Voice.

The BOSUN goes.

CABIN-BOY: Will he wake?

The SURGEON shrugs, takes the bottle and repacks his bag.

SURGEON: Every Man should ask that of himself before he makes the Voyage. If he never surfaces – a dark God of Pain has pulled him under.

The SURGEON stands with his things.

                              Keep Watch. Until Morning. If he re-gains … Reason … he'll open his Eyes onto an Ocean of Light.

The SURGEON turns and goes.

                              That Reason rises at all is a perpetual Miracle.

The CABIN-BOY fetches a canvas awning and covers TOM. He brings the oil-lamp nearer and huddles up against him. The sound of the sea, of the ship's movement. The BOSUN enters quietly, puts out the oil-lamp, and beckons the CABIN-BOY.

SCENE ELEVEN

Tactics

TARLETON and WILBERFORCE meet across the committee-table.

WIBERFORCE: Abolition, Mr Tarleton. Some Propose a
               Regulation of the Trade? A Restriction, say, to
               one Slave per Ton of Shipping?

TARLETON: If a Ship of 200 Ton does not purchase 400
               Slaves and more, she sinks her Owner's Money.
               And besides, Space for the Slaves varies not
               according to Tonnage, but the Beam of the Ship.
               Shall I go on? Profit, Mr Wilberforce, is spoken
               in the Language of Arithmetic. The Measures
               being put forward of a Regulation of our Ships
               are a Nonsense, with no Language to them at
               all, but an Enmity to Trade.

WILBERFORCE: I can only agree. Let us not press any further on
               Regulation.

*A Bell rings for the start of the committee. FOX enters, and takes his place
beside WIBERFORCE, who leans over and whispers into his ear – FOX nods.*

FOX: You are John Tarleton, Esquire; a Merchant in
               the African Trade?

TARLETON: I am.

FOX: When a Merchant boards his Ship, does he
               calculate how many Slaves it can reasonably
               accommodate?

TARLETON: It must be left to the Captain's Discretion. He knows how many Slaves can accommodate a Profit.

FOX: Are Slaves ever confined in a Place where they cannot stand upright?

TARLETON: At Night, when they go to sleep, we do not intend they should stand upright, but that they should lie down.

FOX: Do you mean they cannot stand upright?

TARLETON: I do.

FOX: Could the tallest of them sit upright in that Space?

TARLETON: Negroes do not sleep in a sitting Posture.

FOX: On Account of Cramp and bad Circulation, are the Negroes ever forced to dance in the Day-Time?

TARLETON: I never saw it necessary to use Force for that Purpose.

FOX: Is Force not the Stock in Trade of a Slave Ship? Are Slaves not fettered by the Ankle, Irons locked to the Wrist to restrain sudden Out-Bursts of Joyousness? Do they not, in fact, dance to the Tune of a Whip?

TARLETON: As you know, Out-Bursts of Joy can be as un-Accountable as Out-Bursts of Bad Humour. The Slaves are made Comfortable, and not cruelly treated.

FOX: Do not their Rooms stink abominably from the Nastiness of the Tubs, and from the Negroes doing what is Necessary on the Platforms and Decks?

TARLETON: I do not know anything that is necessary for them to do on the Platforms and Decks. And with respect to the Tubs, there are Lids on 'em.

FOX: Are the Circumstances of being chained, of not having Room to sit, stand or, indeed, lay on their Backs; of Sea-Sickness, Wounds from their Shackles, Confinement between Decks all Night in a fetid Atmosphere and tropical Climate, and being kept there all Day when the Weather is bad, with Disease rife among them – are these not Species of Cruelty?

TARLETON: The Ocean is Cruel not because we make it so, but because it is. If you took the Trouble to observe our Country's Progress in Navigation, Commerce, Opulence and Power, you will find it in fairly exact Proportion to our pursuit of the African Trade. We have brought a Light to that Ocean; the Light of Trade. And clustered our own Mariners about a Brazier of Ship's Coal. But – if it is now thought proper, from Motives of more refined Humanity, to abolish the Slave Trade – then, we, the African Merchants of Liverpool, Bristol and London, desire to be paid Compensation for the Loss of all we have Staked.

An uncomfortable silence.

WILBERFORCE: Very well. Thank you, Mr Tarleton. We shall adjourn.

TARLETON: Gentlemen.

TARLETON stands and goes.

WIBERFORCE: Regulation I knew he'd solicit. Then oppose. But Compensation, that's new. He moves fast.

FOX: What Speculation in the City, Mr Wilberforce?

WIBERFORCE turns to FOX, coolly.

85

I hear some want an Abolition of this Trade because they see India as the Prize and want protection for that. Others again, your Hull merchants, in the Baltic Trade, make claim for competing Subsidy to deal in fish, seal-oil and furs. Yet more – but this annoys me – have their Eye on a more thorough Exploitation of Africa's People and Resources than any Slave affords.

WIBERFORCE: It is not our Task to block the Traffic in and out of Trade, Mr Fox. Our Aim's to abolish a Trafficking of Slaves. An Alliance of Motives – some pure, others not so – but Purification of Trade, that it might flow more freely, and with less Guilt, is something, surely, on which we can all agree? More Light upon the Oceans. Let us not exclude Africa because she is Dark.

FOX: Is Moral Scruple now the Dog of Profit? Does it bark and growl and settle at the Feet of Cash?

WILBERFORCE: I am indeed the Member for Hull; put there for a Purpose. And by God, you wrong me. *(More coolly)* This is the last Session of the Committee in its present Form.

FOX: Sir?

WIBERFORCE: It's Time we argued our Case before a Committee of the Whole House of Parliament. Or do we want to rake over these Ashes of Evidence forever?

FOX: I suppose you have set a Date for it?

WILBERFORCE: Pitt, and the City, will bring it on.

FOX: I am certain of Nothing.

WILBERFORCE stands, and goes.

WIBERFORCE: Which is why we must press on.

FOX shuts his book.

SCENE TWELVE

The Abolition of Sin

The breaking grey storm-light of early morning. TOM lying alone; he doesn't move, but his eyes are open.
The SURGEON stumbles in, drunk, carrying an oil-lamp and a bottle. He stops abruptly in the half-light, hearing TOM struggle to move under the canvas.

SURGEON: Who's there?

TOM: Help me ...

He approaches TOM – finds him conscious and sobbing.

SURGEON: Here, Man. You've had a Hurt. Go easy.

The SURGEON cradles TOM's head and tries to make him drink. TOM raises an arm to ward it off and draw the SURGEON nearer.

TOM: The killing ... I saw ...

The SURGEON shakes his head wearily.

SURGEON: I'm not your Confessor. We're all Slavers here.

TOM: I saw ... The Bosun – shot me ... He saw ... and shot me.

TOM collapses back into the SURGEON's arms.
Shaking his head, the SURGEON raises his bottle.

SURGEON: We are beyond help.

The BOSUN enters, pushing the CABIN-BOY from behind, forward onto the deck.

BOSUN: *(To TOM)* Still here?

The BOSUN takes out JENNY's necklace in full view of TOM.

         (To the CABIN-BOY) Come here, Girl!

The CABIN-BOY is pulled roughly to face TOM and the SURGEON. The BOSUN fixes the necklace around the CABIN-BOY's neck, keeping his hands around the throat and shoulders.

         Doesn't she look pretty?

The SURGEON stands unsteadily.

SURGEON: Leave your Blood-Lust!

BOSUN: *(To the CABIN-BOY)* They're only Jealous. They'll turn into Wet-Fish, and we'll turn into Otters and Hunt 'em down.

The SURGEON swings at the BOSUN with the bottle. The BOSUN dodges it easily and knocks him down. The CAPTAIN enters with JAKE.

CAPTAIN: Who's creating here?

The CAPTAIN goes over to the SURGEON, takes the bottle from his hand and smells it. He looks at the SURGEON.

         You again? Thought I'd knocked that Devil out of you. *(To JAKE and the BOSUN)* Hang him out to dry in the Rigging.

They lay hold of the SURGEON, concussed, drunk and confused.

SURGEON: Damn you!

CAPTAIN: Damn me, is it? Haul him up! *(To the CABIN-BOY)* Fetch the Whip! *(To the BOSUN)* Twenty strokes to the Gore.

JAKE and the BOSUN drag the SURGEON out. The CABIN-BOY looks to TOM, who stares back at his necklace.

Go, Boy!

The CABIN-BOY goes. The CAPTAIN looks down at TOM.

There's no more he can do for you.

The CAPTAIN turns to go, TOM struggles to sit up.

TOM: Wrong ... Captain ... You're Wrong ...

CAPTAIN: I will keep Discipline, I will keep Order aboard my Ship.

TOM: The Devil's aboard ...

The CAPTAIN steps up to TOM.

CAPTAIN: Were it not for your Uncle, I would have *you* whipped.

TOM: For God's Sake ... Stop ... What you do is Wrong ...

CAPTAIN: I know you a Coward; I see you also a Fool. Should I not protect my Ship? Were we not Attacked; did we not Reply? What say you?

TOM: On my Conscience ... I cannot ...

CAPTAIN: My Boy, I drag along in my Chest, having the Sea by heart, and an honest Terror of it. It has put the Fear of God in his Face. I see it there. Look yours be not Marred by the Sin of Revolt.

The sound of a whip – and one short cry from the CABIN-BOY – then nothing.

TOM: He misleads you ... Your Bosun ... The Devil's in *him*...

CAPTAIN: What do you know of the Devil, Boy? Are you

turned now a creeping, Insolent Cat; that you smell the Rat at work in a Barrel? No more talk to me of Wrong than the Devil. My God guides my Feet, on Land and Sea.

TOM: By Murder ... At large ... Are you Blind?

The CAPTAIN steps on and grinds TOM's wounds.

CAPTAIN: Aye, lie in your Wounds; let them corrupt. You may as well whip the Devil from a Dead Man's Skin as abolish Sin.

TOM: I am paying for my Sins ... Paying for them ... Put that to my Name!

CAPTAIN: I have but one Name for a whole Continent of Fellows such as you, marked out on my Charts, and squared with my Employer – that's the Slave Coast. There is no End to its Sickness. Sin it is; and since it is, sick unto their Souls, Men shall suffer to be Slaves –

Rumbling sound of a rolling barrel. JAKE enters.

(*To JAKE*) What's there?

JAKE: The Surgeon hung by the Wrists, but the Boy whipped – bringing the wrong one. The Boy's hid from the Bosun in a Barrel. Men say, the World turns ... but the Sun stands still. (*Points at TOM*) We took a Hurt, and got no Slaves. Got a bloody Mouth – Loose Teeth. Ill Luck. Let roll –

The BOSUN enters, rolling a barrel, his shirt off and the whip bloody in his hand.

CAPTAIN: (*Shouts*) Stop that!

The BOSUN pushes the barrel forward. The CABIN-BOY crawls out to hide under TOM's canvas.

(To the BOSUN) I'll be damned if I don't break you!

BOSUN: Brought him before you, Sir. The Lad brought a Lash to dance the Man – not the Cat Tail.

CAPTAIN: Dampen down. Get below among the Slaves and see them properly stowed for the Crossing. I'll deal with this.

The BOSUN bows his head, looks at TOM, and goes.

(To TOM) Your Key, Sir.

JAKE leaps to seize it from TOM's pocket.

(To JAKE) Go cut down the Surgeon. And give each man his Guinea.

The CAPTAIN goes.

I'll be in my Cabin.

JAKE: *(To TOM)* He means to Curse; he offers Money.

TOM: You're his Boy …

JAKE: I'm his Slave. Wake up – You Dream.

TOM slumps back on the deck. The CABIN-BOY crawls sobbing under TOM's arm.

TOM: *(To the CABIN-BOY)* Not a Sound … Keep still … We're at Sea …

JAKE: Deeper still – you wake and find yourself a Slaver; she wakes below, that Child, sees where she is, and Screams, in Chains. Does that not shake you?

JAKE goes.

SCENE THIRTEEN

The Crypt Chapel of the Palace of Westminster

TARLETON enters with WILBERFORCE.

WILBERFORCE: A God-fearing man, Mr Tarleton?

TARLETON: I cannot doubt the sincerity of your Convictions
                 or Motives; I hope you will not doubt mine.
                 Money is a jealous God I appease when I can.

WILBERFORCE: Perhaps in every Generation, some few still
                 manage to ride the Dragon of their Sins, at the
                 last Moment, recanting into Sainthood. In the
                 City, of course, they all do Business together
                 – the Jew, the Christian, the Mohammedan –
                 as though they were all of one Religion. The
                 one whom they call 'Infidel' is he who goes
                 bankrupt.

TARLETON: You wished to see me privately, Mr Wilberforce?

WILBERFORCE: The Mob – both here in the House and in the
                 Country – is against you. Money will take its
                 Course in a more profitable Exploitation of
                 Africa than Slavery. A Course – less bloody.

TARLETON: Blood? I see no Blood. We are One Nation, Mr
                 Wilberforce; we are not killing each other like
                 the French.

WIBERFORCE: The Country demands Consensus – that we

should turn our Blood-letting against France, not sell them Slaves. Strength through Trade is the Secret of War. Who controls Trade of the most Vigorous and Profitable sort will emerge the Victor in our inevitable Conflict. The Slave Trade does not pay, it is an Impediment, an Obstruction – and that, for a Nation at War, is unforgivable. Whereas – the Word 'Credit' is yet to be found in the African Dictionary. Think only of its Potential as a market for our Manufactures; its Raw Wealth yet to be brought to the Light of a free Trade. It is this new Trade that will work for us and against the blood-guilt of France.

TARLETON: For *us*, Mr Wilberforce?

WIBERFORCE: If this more humane Trade is to thrive, it is to the Masters of the African Trade we must turn. They alone can exchange the hard Currency of Slaves for the Vigour of a new Employment. Think on it, Mr Tarleton. You would have the support of this Government.

TARLETON: Abolition, Mr Wilberforce? Of the Trade, or of Slavery itself?

WIBERFORCE: Slavery is repugnant to me. And bad for Business. It is likely the House may take a long View of abolishing it.

TARLETON: We were not Devils, Mr Wilberforce, to ride so hard our Investments in the Trade.

TARLETON bows, and goes.

WILBERFORCE: Don't give up without a Struggle. The Mob must have Blood – must catch the Scent and get a Taste for it, if Slavery is to be absolved in War.

He goes.

SCENE FOURTEEN

Peace at Sea

The NEGER SHANTYMAN sits squat over a Corpse sewn into a Hammock,
an oil-lamp hung directly overhead, casting shadow on his face.
He throws down 4 cowrie shells, and nods – "Oyeku Meji!"
He darns another four double stitches into the Shroud over the Corpse's face.

NEGER SHANTYMAN:

> *Says Jack, There is very good News;*
> *There is Peace both by Land and Sea;*
> *Great Guns no more shall be used,*
> *For we all disbanded must be.*
>
> *Says the Merchant, That's very bad News.*
> *Says the Captain, My Heart will break.*
> *O! says the bloody Bosun,*
> *What Course of Life shall I take?*
>
> *Says the Surgeon, I'm a Gentleman born,*
> *A Gent of the very first Rank;*
> *I will go to some Country Fair and there*
> *I'll set up Stall as a Quack.*
>
> *Says the Carpenter, I have a Chest,*
> *A Chest of very good Tools;*
> *I will go away to some Country Fair*
> *And sell three-legged Stools.*
>
> *Says the Purser, I have my Doubts,*
> *I'd lose at Cards or at Dice;*

> *Should I jump from the Side of the Ship and let*
> *The Salt-Water flash in my Eyes?*
>
> *Says Jack, I will take to the Road,*
> *For I'd better do that than do Worse;*
> *And for everyone that comes I'll cry,*
> *Damn you, Deliver your Purse!*

He rises, extinguishes the oil lamp to daylight and goes.

Talk about the Weather

The CAPTAIN enters, the BOSUN following.

CAPTAIN:	Open the hatches. Bring up the Slaves – chains, bolts and shackles.
BOSUN:	We've work to keep them Chained down, Captain. The Weather still – they grow suspicious.
CAPTAIN:	And clear that off the Deck.
BOSUN:	*(Calling off)* You there, bring Rope.
CAPTAIN:	What do the Men mutter?
BOSUN:	Captain?
CAPTAIN:	What do they tell you?
BOSUN:	They become Silent.

JAKE and the CABIN-BOY enter with rope for the Body.

CAPTAIN:	Your Debt is cancelled on Signature. My signature, once we dock. Have you some other way to go free? Bend to your Task, Bosun. What's the Weather?
BOSUN:	We've hit the Calms – they feel it. So do the Slaves. The Current stalled. No Wind to keep

us steady in the long Swells – masts and Yards creaking and jerking, Sails flapping at every Roll – what's to say this Dog of a corpse, floating on Water, won't Shake us more with its Ghost?

CAPTAIN: *(To JAKE)* Weight the body. *(To the CABIN-BOY)* Fetch Ballast.

The CABIN-BOY goes; JAKE ropes the Body.

And give this Man his Due; he makes a Sacrifice. Keep them Steady, Bosun; I'll lose no more Men.

BOSUN: Aye, Sir.

CAPTAIN: What do *you* Smell in the Wind?

BOSUN: What wind, Sir?

CAPTAIN: Without it you will never go Free.

BOSUN: So – I smell Good Hope, Captain.

CAPTAIN: As you should; so should every Christian. *(Taking grit from his tongue)* Feel that? Grit. There's Sand in it. I know I smell Wind. This Air's a Calm before a Storm, Mr Palmer. It's a Desert, blowing out of Africa.

BOSUN: On your Word, Sir.

CAPTAIN: Aye. I saw it once before – a dust cloud, orange Light. There's a Wind coming. We'll be moving. Back to Life, from the late Disorders. All Hangs on my Word. Won't it, Bosun?

BOSUN: Aye, Sir.

CAPTAIN: Bring the Slaves up in Gangs. Let them get their Breath.

BOSUN: *(To JAKE)* Clear the Way.

The CAPTAIN and BOSUN go.
As JAKE fastens a knot, the CABIN-BOY returns with rock Ballast. They
fasten it together as TOM enters silently, supporting himself.

JAKE: Come to your own Drowning?

JAKE gives hold of the rope to TOM, and follows after the CAPTAIN.
The CABIN-BOY looks at TOM.

CABIN-BOY: Say something?

TOM shakes his head.

                          He saved you.

TOM: Slip him down, so he won't know a thing.

They lift and push the hammock overboard. A silence; no splash.

CABIN-BOY: When you die, you go to Heaven. When you
                          die at Sea, you're sewn into your Hammock and
                          thrown to the Fish. You're adrift, and no-one
                          gives a damn.

TOM sits, leans back, looks up. The sound of wind being taken in canvas.

TOM: A Wing-flap in the Sails – is that his Soul?

The CABIN-BOY takes out a knife and scores the man's initials on the deck.

CABIN-BOY: *All dank his Hair, all dim his Eyes,*
                          I'm nine Days drifting with the Tide.
                          Lowlands, lowlands away, my Boys,
                          My Lowlands away.

                          All green and wet with Hands so cold,
                          About his Arms the Weeds take hold.
                          Lowlands, lowlands away, my Boys,
                          My Lowlands away.

> *I will cut my Clothes until they bleed,*
> *His Form is gone in the green Weed.*
> *My Love lies drowned in the windy Lowlands,*
> *My Love lies drowned in the windy Lowlands.*

The sound of a Wind builds, the flap of Sail; the CAPTAIN enters with a musket.

CAPTAIN: See how they like a Wind after their Confinement! I don't care if the Devil blows! Bring up the Negroes!

Sound of a hatch flung open. A short rattling of chains, then silence. The CAPTAIN paces, ignoring all except the sound of Wind clutching Canvas. But the silence brings him back.

                     What have you?

BOSUN (Off):   Avoid your Eyes!

The BOSUN dragging JAKE after him, both armed – they sprawl to the deck, drenched in sweat.

CAPTAIN: What's this?

JAKE: They have the Blind God!

The BOSUN shakes the sweat from his eyes, wipes his face with his arm, stops and looks at his hands.

BOSUN: They spat in our Eyes!

CAPTAIN: What is it, Man?

BOSUN: The Blindness is spread among them.

CAPTAIN: Blind? *(Calling out)* Close the Hatches! Shut them down; keep the Crew away!

TOM clutches the CABIN-BOY, recoiling from the sprawled bodies.
Sound of the hatch banged shut; wind blowing stronger, as storm-light darkens.

JAKE: *(To the CAPTAIN)* We have no Surgeon.

The CAPTAIN looks up into the sky.

CAPTAIN: This Storm will blow over.

He turns to go. He stops, facing away.

                        Blind?

He goes.

TOM: *(Calling to JAKE)* What with their Eyes? What is it?

JAKE looks at him, does not respond; rises and follows after the CAPTAIN.
The BOSUN stands, gathers his breath.

BOSUN: It's a Fire. No one escapes. Sometimes, in one
                        Eye, sometimes both. You may recover. But if
                        the Brain catches Fire – how much for a Cargo
                        of Corpses, Purser? *(To the CABIN-BOY)* Go
                        below, put out all Fires; Hands to the Storm, it
                        approaches.

The CABIN-BOY goes.

                        (To TOM) When you are very Blind, I will Shoot
                        you in the Eye.

The BOSUN turns and goes, shouting to the Crew.

                        You Stand and Stare, you Dogs! All Hands,
                        Reeving and Furling; Shake your Ghosts! Now
                        is for Battening down!

A sound of thunder.
Blinking, TOM ropes himself in, and watches.

SCENE FIFTEEN

Blind Rage

The deck of the ship in the Storm transforms as FOX enters and exchanges glances with TOM. TARLETON enters, glances across at TOM and joins the assembly in exchanges with WILBERFORCE as the ship's crew mingles blindly with Members in what becomes the aisle of the House. FOX speaks into uproar.

FOX: This pestilential *Disease* has spread through the Dregs of the People! Its *Infectious Air* has wafted into this very Chamber – for even here, strange to say, Slavery has found *Abettors!* Do I Slander honest Men, intent on stealing their Property? That a majority should hold this Traffic so tenaciously, with their Eyes open on its Guilt, and refuse to let it go!

BOSUN: Clew in and Make Fast! Damn you, Haul!

TARLETON: Our Families, our Fortunes are at Stake.

CAPTAIN: The Sea rises against us! Look to the Helm!

TARLETON: As our Lives; we defend them.

FOX: You cannot Look! Interest has spread a Film over the Eyes thick enough to occasion total Blindness!

CAPTAIN: Keep her Bow to the Wave! Pray God she Holds!

WILBERFORCE: Do you presume a cool indifference, and continue a Criminal Practice?

TARLETON: Do you claim this long-established Struggle with the Waves has not been Lawful?

CAPTAIN: Keep going that Chain-Pump – to the Bilge! She takes too much Water!

WILBERFORCE: It admits no Cure; it is a Sinking Ship.

TARLETON: Not Lawful?

FOX: What is *their* Crime that Slaves lie below in Chains? – *Gone, lost*, you say, in a Swamp of Sin! The Shriek of a Salamander among a Tangle of Roots that was Africa! – But *your* Crime remains whole and entire in Every One of you! – Oh, there is uproar! I can hear! – When Trade is at Stake it is your last Retrenchment; you must defend it, or perish!

BOSUN: Must our mouths be Cold?

CAPTAIN: *(To TOM)* Go your Way – Go all of you within, for any Good you have done!

TOM goes, the assembly dissolves. FOX and WILBERFORCE stand alone.

WILBERFORCE: The Slave Trade is one Scene of Silence and Devastation. White and Black are all corruptly traumatised by it. But now is not the Time for self-inflicted Wounds. No Eloquence will move the Armies of France from our Coast.

FOX: You do abandon Hope of ever seeing Slavery abolished?

WILBERFORCE: You have lit the Path to a gradual Abolition.

FOX: In a Gale of Wind? A nearer Means to preserve Slavery in its Death Agonies forever!

WIBERFORCE: Rage will pass; and so will Slavery. Mr Fox.
                     Until it is Water under the Bridge.

WILBERFORCE turns and walks away.

FOX: I will abandon this Struggle only with my Breath!

WILBERFORCE: *(Nods)* One whom God burnt with an Angry
                     Heart.

He goes.

FOX: If my Mouth be cold, who will Speak for me
                     before my God?

*The NEGER SHANTYMAN emerges from shadow, to place a Guinea in
FOX's mouth.*

NEGER SHANTYMAN: We are made of life and death.

FOX grasps it and goes.
The SHANTYMAN lifts his arms in peril of the storm.

SCENE SIXTEEN

The Accounting

TOM sits within, writing into the ship's book. A door blows open in the storm; he looks up, with unseeing eyes.

TOM: Who's there?

He rubs his eyes, brings nearer the light of the tallow and peers back at the book to write, feeling the page.

> *(Reads)* "… The Storm then not abating, we were borne helpless away –"

JAKE falls inside, exhausted from the storm, and feels his way to shelter – without TOM looking up from the page.

> Who is it?

JAKE stops, raising his head to listen – he can't see – and doesn't respond.

> I see. *(Writes aloud)* "Now all the Crew are Blind, or nearly Blind. But one Man –"

JAKE: Make mention – in your Papers – The Cat – The Cat sees – into the crawling Spaces – the darkest Corners of the Ship – seems in hissing almost to Speak … Leave out no Detail – The black Cat, with Green Eyes – Let it speak – what blinded Rats do here for meat – among the Creatures you despise.

TOM: Why do you hate me?

JAKE: You Despise yourself – What hope for me?

TOM: *(Shrugs)* None I know of.

TOM resumes writing.

"… The Captain is Blind, standing by with a Rope to thrash any Man he is led to by the Man who can see. We are Blind, Stone-Blind. Each of us lives in a small dark world of his Sins. My own eyes begin to be affected. In a while, I shall see nothing but Death –"

JAKE: *(Laughter)* Now the Earth, the Sea, all things are giving up their Dead – you Begin to see?

TOM: I see you – among Shadows crowding the Deck. The Captain's steady, sullen Shadow, as though you were drowned and dead already.

JAKE: You see me? A blurred Shadow, committed to Memory? *(Nods)* Before ever I lost my Eyes, I saw the Skin and Sinews of this Trade – You have not seen what I have seen. You cannot write it – I am a Blot on your Papers.

TOM: Ink has its Purpose. How come you into the Account? A Stain on the Captain's Conscience. A Slave he puts to do his Work in Darkness. Of whom he will never be free.

JAKE: He longs for Death – to go free. It is his Religion. But I can't save him; he is my Father, he owns me. Make good your Escape, Purser, flee us now … we are Shackled.

The BOSUN enters from the storm with a knotted rope.

TOM: Who's that?

BOSUN: Blind?

TOM: Not yet!

The CAPTAIN staggers in, blind and soaked, a wreck.

CAPTAIN: Who hides from the Storm? *(To the BOSUN)*
                         Give him a Taste of the Rope's End!

The BOSUN whirls the rope and thrashes JAKE, who recoils from the blow.

BOSUN: *(To the Captain)* It's the Purser – bent on his Book.

*The CAPTAIN staggers towards TOM, who falls from his chair, cowering from
a blow. The CAPTAIN feels his way over and touches him.*

CAPTAIN: Can you write?

TOM: Yes.

CAPTAIN: Then write this.

*The CAPTAIN guides TOM back to his chair. TOM feels for his pen and the
book.*

                         When Time comes to log a narrative of the
                         Voyage – and make Account – there will be
                         Gaps, out of which the Storm came. Are you
                         ready?

TOM: Yes.

CAPTAIN: I, John Knox, Master of the *Black'moor Jenny*,
                         being Blind in my Eyes but of Sound Mind …
                         (Shakes his head) That's a Will … It blowing hard
                         at South, and being thick, dirty Weather and
                         grown Sea … we unbent our Cables and cleared
                         our Ship …

TOM listens, making no further attempt to write; the BOSUN watches.

                         We hauled up our Main-Sails, clapt the helm
                         a-weather, and bore away under Fore-Sails and
                         Main Top-Sail … In furling our Main-Sail one
                         of our Sea-Men, being careless of himself, fell
                         off the Yard-Arm and was drowned …

TOM feels his way out to the storm, while the CAPTAIN continues. The BOSUN whispers to TOM as he passes.

BOSUN: Blind?

TOM goes.

CAPTAIN: ... It was beyond Human Power to save him. It blowing a Gale of Wind, and a very great Sea ...

The BOSUN readies a pistol and follows TOM out, leaving JAKE alone listening silently to the CAPTAIN.

> The Blindness coming at last upon us, We went to bring to under a Mizzen; but in Hauling out our Mizzen the Strap of the Sheet-Block broke, so that ever before we could brail him up he was by the Violence of the Storm split to Pieces. And we were forced to bear away before the Wind – You hear me?

The CAPTAIN listens, no response.

> Our Cargo in Chains, our Souls rotting. The Ocean swept us away. And without Men, the Ocean disappeared from View. We pulled on an Oar, and the World was gone.

The CABIN-BOY enters, stumbling.

> Who's there? Jake?

CABIN-BOY: *(Looking at JAKE)* Only me. Only for a Rest.

CAPTAIN: The Boy? O! That's young. What Rest? When I rose in the morning, and shook myself like a Dog, I was dressed.

CABIN-BOY: It's Cold, Sir.

CAPTAIN: Are your Fingers grown hard, Boy, and tarry with hauling all day on the Ropes?

CABIN-BOY: I can't see. I can feel them.

CAPTAIN: Would like a Slave, instead?

CABIN-BOY: Aye!

CAPTAIN: What would you do with him?

CABIN-BOY: Why, feed him.

CAPTAIN: That's right. To make him Strong. But you'd
                   make him work, wouldn't you?

CABIN-BOY: Aye, to be sure!

CAPTAIN: Then you must Flog him as well as feed him.

CABIN-BOY: I will. Not to hurt too much …

CAPTAIN: No, not to Death. Not to Maim him. Then he'd
                   not work. But if you'd not make him feel to the
                   Marrow, you might as well throw him to the
                   Sea.

The CAPTAIN goes, blindly feeling his way.

CABIN-BOY: *(To JAKE)* What does he say?

No response.

                   Should I let go the Slaves?

JAKE: There is no Forgiveness. There is a Book here
                   on this table? – How do you See?

CABIN-BOY: In one Eye – nearly.

JAKE: Can you Read?

CABIN-BOY: No.

JAKE: Then take that Book, and throw it in the Sea.

JAKE climbs to his feet and follows out after the CAPTAIN.
The CABIN-BOY opens and feels the pages of the book.

CABIN-BOY: What does it say? Are there Pictures? Does it
sing?

A shot. The CABIN-BOY flinches. Another shot.

What's your Fortune, pretty Maid?
My Face is my Fortune, Sir, she said.
What's that Wind that takes my Breath?
Death, Sir, Death, Sir, Death, Sir, Death.

He takes the book and goes.

SCENE SEVENTEEN

Succession

JENNY walks in the rain with TARLETON along George's Dock in Liverpool.

JENNY: In such a Storm, I have heard tell of a Spectre,
                           the Ghost of a full-rigged Ship in full Sail –
                           white, transparent – how suddenly it looms in
                           the black Darkness, tearing along on a reckless
                           Course, all her Sails and Gear aloft plainly
                           Visible. Are we come to that? Our lost Ship
                           a Terror and a Danger to Ordinary, decent
                           Seamen? I shudder to think how long we have
                           waited.

They walk on in silence.

                           What News?

TARLETON: Some un-Accountable Trouble on the Coast.
                           There is no News of his Arrival in the West
                           India Islands.

JENNY: I am not his Widow. News of Mr Pitt?

TARLETON: *(Absorbs the change)* The Motion for an Abolition
                           has failed. Yet the Business will no longer
                           expand; Investment will dwindle, the City will
                           see to that.

JENNY: How will you respond?

TARLETON: There will be War with France. Pitt must have Armies, and they must have Supplies: Wool, Gun Metal, Powder – Meat and Drink.

JENNY takes a ball of dyed Indian silk from her coat and hands it to him.

JENNY: Money also comes from India, in Cotton, Silks and Spices. I'll see to that. Madras, Calcutta, Bombay – names to conjure as old ones fade from the Accounts – we'll quite forget Old Calabar, the Slave and Gold Coasts, the Island of Goree. There's also Opium for that. Trade moves on, and so must we.

They look at each other.

TARLETON: I see.

He hands it back. JENNY toys with the ball of silk.

JENNY: A World opens ... a world closes.

TARLETON: We should seek the privacy of the Rain more often.

They walk on along the Docks, sailors passing.

NEGER SHANTYMAN:

> *O, I thought I heard the Old Man say*
> *Leave her, Johnny, leave her,*
> *For Tomorrow ye will get your Pay*
> *And it's Time for us to leave her!*

SHANTY CHORUS:

> *Well the Rats are gone and we the Crew,*
> *Leave her, Johnny, leave her,*
> *O, I think by God, that we'll go too!*
> *And it's Time for us to leave her!*
>
> *Pray that me ye never see,*
> *Leave her, Johnny, leave her,*

Not the hungry Bitch the likes o' she!
And it's Time for us to leave her!

Belay!

~END~